MW01715737

Compassionate Birth

for you and your baby

Credit to Amber Kuhn Photography

Di Bustamante, CH, DBLE, PPNE, CD

ISBN 978-1-63784-340-6 (paperback)
ISBN 978-1-63784-341-3 (digital)

Hawes & Jenkins Publishing
16427 N Scottsdale Road Suite 410
Scottsdale, AZ 85254
www.hawesjenkins.com

Printed in the United States of America

CONTENTS

INTRODUCTION

It was suggested to me by a friend who reviewed my first draft that I explain my book, why I wrote it, and who my audience should be. So here we go.

I wanted to reach out to parents who were planning a pregnancy or unexpectedly found themselves with a pending birthing. With my first baby, I was so unaware of pregnancy, labor, and birth. I had no idea how my own birth experience—when I was born—could affect how I would carry my babies, how I would birth them, and how I would parent them. It's been quite a journey to get to where I am today, wanting to share my story and what I have learned so others can have a more straightforward pathway.

My story will also aid those who have experienced sexual abuse as children and have been influenced in unknown ways. All our life experiences—starting with our time in the womb—shape our belief systems and, ultimately, our reactions, interactions, relationships, and decision-making processes.

I've outlined my childhood sexual encounters with a broad brushstroke so I would not shock or create a negative response from those also dealing with PTSD from childhood abuse. On my first pass at this book, I went into minute details only to realize that while this might be cathartic for me, it most likely would not add value to others' reading and learning experiences.

I hope to reach the maternity care providers out there who have not yet made the leap to look at birth as a normal physiological event—to care for mothers by being with them, not controlling the pregnancy, labor, and birthing but by being conscious of the awareness of the baby within and the newborn. This is vital if we want to create gentle and loving human beings.

I want to thank everyone who has supported me, put up with me, mentored me, and loved me along the way, including but not limited to my son and daughter. They have taught me so much more than I have ever taught them. My partner for the hours I have spent on my computer. My friends that reviewed my drafts of this book. The lovely parents I have supported as a doula, taught childbirth classes to, and those mothers willing to share their birth experiences. Colleagues who have grown with me every step of the way. Those who have mentored me in everything birthing and parenting.

Much gratitude to Xenia Black Pettigrew, Oli Pettigrew, Charlie Schudson, Jennifer Norris, Wes Caldwell, Sophia Bustamante, Bill Caldwell, Jennie Blake, Jo Teo, Tan Kay Yen, Megan Tan, Claudine Cerrani, David Austin, Jen Tsai, Ginny Phang, Mairead Furlong, Nikki McFarlane, Tania Hodge, Dr. Lai Fon Min, Professor Chong Yap Seng, Deb Fox, Dr. Park Jie Won, Mickey Mongan, Kim Wildner, Kim Young, Vivian Keeler, Eileen Goh, Dr. Paul Tseng, Claudia Khoo, George Bettis, Elena Tonetti, Dr. Laura Maurer, Dr. Deibby Mamahit, and for all those willing to share their birth stories.

SECTION 1

A Small Step in the Right Direction

In 2013, I was invited to speak at the Obstetrics and Gynecological Conference in Singapore, and I was provided with twenty minutes. I decided that my presentation would be on what babies want—how babies want to be born. I had much information to pack into that short time frame. It would be a new perspective for most obstetricians and obstetric nurses. I remember being a bit nervous, as I wanted the presentation to be credible to the medical community. After working for ten years in this field, I knew how they tended to avoid the emotional aspect of birthing and focused solely on the medical training. They are dismissive of compassionate birthing.

I was previously invited to speak by Dr. Chong Yap Seng at an in-house training session for all the maternity and postnatal ward staff at Singapore National University Hospital. Dr. Chong introduced midwifery care and water birthing at National University Hospital. My topic was on different positions to labor and birth and why they would create a better outcome for mothers and babies. I showed my video, *Birth Move*Ment,* created by midwives in Germany; there was quite a buzz. Dr. Chong stood up to interrupt the chatter. Even though this was not what they had learned in school, he requested to listen with an open mind. He had seen the positive results of my efforts with birth movement, using different positions during labor to ease the baby moving through the pelvis. I found it quite amazing, as the first question following the film and presentation was about doulas, not the presentation's content. A doctor asked about doulas interfering at births. I explained that it is not a doula's role to interfere but to offer emotional and informational support. The head of both departments asked me why women wanted doulas anyway. Ah, bless him for the asking! I thanked him generously for asking this pertinent question. And then I told them.

Firstly, oxytocin, a love hormone, is one of the main hormones in labor. Birth, after all, is part of our reproductive system. There is a sexual element in birthing. Women need the same environment to labor quickly and gently as when they created this miracle. Oxytocin likes privacy and warm, comfortable room temperatures. Women need to feel safe and uninhibited to move about as they please and make the primal noises they innately know they need to make.

According to *A History of Birth* by Tina Cassidy, women had women attending to their births throughout history. Aristotle and Hippocrates stated that women are not sick and did not require physicians unless there were unusual circumstances. They initiated the midwifery approach to supporting women through pregnancy, labor, and birth. In BC times, women averaged four-hour labors. They were not afraid; they trusted their maternity care providers. It was not understood that men had anything to do with procreation in those days. Women were thought to be quite miraculous for their ability to bring forth life. There were rituals surrounding birth, and the midwives sought to comfort and connect with the pregnant woman. They stayed with her throughout her entire labor and helped her postnatally. These healing women were a commanding presence within their communities and sought for advice and counsel.

Constantine the Great shifted away from this approach in AD times, as he embraced a new religion. To wrest power away from these women, they were deemed witches. Hundreds of thousands of these supportive, knowledgeable, and caring women were killed.

With the wise women gone, there was no sharing of information about childbirth. If there were challenges during labor, women died. Only sheepherders were allowed to attend these births to save the baby via cesareans. Martin Luther stated, "Let the women die; that's what they are there for." Women were now fearful, and labor

began to last much longer. According to ACOG (American College of Obstetrics and Gynecologists), labor averages fifteen to eighteen hours of active labor today.

Queen Elizabeth demanded that she be given chloroform for her birthings, and this is when births shifted from home to hospital. Doctors were now allowed to attend births. Protocols were developed, and unfortunately, they did not include the emotional side of birthing. The sacredness surrounding birth was excluded, only focusing on the ease and comfort of medical staff.

In the present day, when women are pregnant, most see their doctor once a month throughout their pregnancy for maybe ten minutes. When in labor, they go to the hospital and are greeted by staff they don't know. The doctor comes in at the end to "catch" the baby.

Women who want doulas want them to bridge this gap. Women crave the intimacy and connection needed throughout their pregnancy, especially during labor. Postnatal care is critical, as women struggle to understand what the baby needs, how to care for themselves as exhaustion sets in, and how to provide attention to their spouses to keep their marriage intact.

There were no further questions after that. The head of departments did comment that I seemed intelligent and well-informed. He wondered why I didn't become a professional and take midwifery training? I could have been annoyed at not already being considered a professional, or I could have been flattered that he thought enough of me to join his clique. I chose to accept the second scenario.

I met the head doctor of the Singapore Obstetrics and Gynecological Association at a workshop I facilitated at one of the local hospitals. The workshop was for the maternity care providers on attending water births safely. I had requested a doula who worked with me to get into the tub to simulate different positions in which to labor and birth. This doctor made a lewd comment about her in her bathing suit. I immediately rebuked him for disrespecting this brave woman and stated that no harassment was allowed. But I had seen this disrespect of actual laboring women many times in my role as a doula.

The head doctor invited me to speak at the annual conference of the Singapore Obstetrics and Gynecological Association. I concluded that the conference would be a great time to address the issue of respecting laboring women.

On a few Facebook new mother pages, I asked what they would want me to share with the doctors about their birth experience that they enjoyed and what they wished could have been different. I was not explicit enough that I only wanted quotes—one-liners. I received a massive outpouring of birth stories—mostly about what had gone pear-shaped (horribly wrong) during their labor. These mothers had wanted gentle births for their babies and were chronologically managed. I asked the mothers if I could use short snippets to share with the doctors.

The speaker scheduled before me at the Singapore conference was a doctor from Scotland. The maternity care providers there are famous for chronologically managing the birth process. He talked about managing the care of all births that came into their hospital in the same way. Only mothers at four centimeters were admitted to the hospital. Once there, all for the first time, mothers were administered Pitocin to speed their labors up.

My presentation covered the importance of respecting women's bodies' ability to labor and birth without medical interference as long as the mother and baby were healthy. I thanked the doctors for having the skills and knowledge to save women when special circumstances required medical intervention.

I continued to describe the hormones of labor and how many medical protocols surrounding childbirth slowed labor down.

I provided evidence-based research on the importance of treating babies gently at birth and respecting the mother-baby dyad.

According to *The Science of Parenting*, babies are born with only 25 percent brain development compared to 45 percent in chimpanzees. Babies have 200 billion brain cells at birth but few connections in the higher brain. The infant's birth experience influences hindbrain and forebrain connections.

If the baby is taken away from the mother and treated roughly, there are more hindbrain connections, enhancing the baby's ability to defend itself right from the start. Those treated gently and allowed to bond with their parents develop more forebrain connections.

I implored the maternity care providers in attendance at the conference to allow women to request and honor natural birth. Birth is, after all, a regular physiological event, not a medical incident.

There was a Q and A session after our talks. The first question was to the Scottish doctor who had presented before me, the one who purported the method of chronologically managing all births.

He was asked, "What do you think about Diann's discussion that women should be allowed natural births?"

Shocking to me, his reply was "Birth is a normal physiological event, and healthy women with healthy babies should be permitted to labor naturally."

I created a one-page handout of quotes from the Facebook mother's groups categorized by what they liked about the maternity care they received, what they wished could have been different, and how they felt about how they were treated. Only one doctor and two nurses picked up the flyer from over two hundred attendees.

I thought about my own birth stories: my two losses in mid-pregnancy and my two children who lived. I wondered how different my experiences would have been having known what I do now.

Stories are only real once they are told. The story can be denied or swept away with time if not told or listened to.

SECTION 2

Right from the Start

I was born in San Diego in the 1950s. My family lived in a quiet little town twenty-five miles inland named Casa de Oro.

Our little "House of Gold" town was about two blocks long. We had a grocery store, Rexall drugstore, appliance store, bar, gas station, laundromat, and an A&W Root Beer stand. Life was lovely growing up in CDO. We left the house right after breakfast and returned for lunch during the summers, only to go again and not show up until supper. Parents did not worry about their children; life was idyllic. Everyone knew each other on the street and many others in the corresponding neighborhoods. We did have one neighbor we avoided because he drank a bit, his yard was unkempt, and his house needed painting. He was a bit scary. One retired neighbor would keep our ball if it went over his fence into his yard. He was a grumpy old guy, and my dad could always be counted on to retrieve it and give the guy a lecture.

The only drawback to the philosophy that all was safe was the troubled soul no one paid attention to. I will not mention names, as anyone involved is unwilling to be part of my telling.

I was a skinny little girl with blue eyes and blond hair and was incredibly shy. I had been born early at thirty-four weeks because my mom was tired of being pregnant, and the doctor was willing to oblige her by inducing her labor, or so my father tells me. I don't think I was quite ready to be born yet—I was underweight—and my mother was a chain-smoker. She said she had stopped having babies, as they kept getting smaller and thought this quite a funny story. No one knew yet that smoking affected babies in the womb. The common belief was that the amniotic sac was a barrier to all harmful influences. My mother told me she had the flu that my eldest sister shared with her after bringing it home from elementary school, and I had moved down sitting on her bladder, which was quite uncomfortable. The doctor suggested induction to end her discomfort. I was a very pale baby and was told I hardly cried.

I avoided crowds. My birthday parties were always overwhelming, and I'd leave to either read a book by myself or watch the party from a distance. Light and sound were too much for me to process. I'd cry when they wanted to take my photo, as I'd have to stare into the sun. Ah, the old Brownie Kodak cameras. I didn't learn how to ride a bike until I was nine. It is not uncommon for preemie babies to be slow in coordination development. Sensory processing disorder was not recognized in those days. Instead of a proper diagnosis, I was labeled as whiny and wimpy. An awkward child at best, I tended to isolate myself, disappearing into the magical world of books. Many games were played on the street during the summers, from hopscotch to marbles and jacks to kick the can and statue maker. The kids from ages five to sixteen seemed to get along, and life was great. I liked to play for hours in the pepper trees in the front yard, fantasizing about pirates and maidens.

I had my tonsils removed at four years, and I remember being very excited about this. I woke up early on the appointed day to pack my bag to take with me. My mother was quite surprised when she got up to see me ready to go. I remember the ward with many beds and other children in them. I was given a presurgical shot of some sort that induced hallucinations. I was sure someone had stolen the pillow from my bed and set out to find it. This activity distressed my mother, as I jumped up to search up and down the rows of beds.

Hospitals were still using ether as an anesthetic at the time. In an outpatient ward setting, my heart and respiration stopped during the surgery. After reviving me, the doctor carried me back into the ward, causing my mother much consternation. I loved the attention at home, with ice chips and popsicles at my beck and call. As an adult, I had a hypnosis session to take me back to the surgery. I recalled the warm yellow color in the surgery room and how caring and concerned the doctor was as he revived me. Later in life, the doctor's loving attention would shadow my ability to make informed decisions, as I always trusted anyone in the medical field.

Soon after the surgery, I was quite vulnerable when a family friend chose to practice foreplay and gain confidence interacting with girls. Boundaries were not set in those days with wee ones. We did what we were told to do by those older than us. He fancied my oldest sister but was too shy to approach her. My sister was and still is stunningly beautiful, Mensa intelligent, charming, and quite witty. This young man was laughed at by his mother for talking to himself. She disciplined him with a wooden spoon that she bonked on his head. He had very low self-esteem, was not very good-looking, and had plenty of acne. He told me I was special and that he and I had our own secret game.

He eventually stopped molesting me, and the last time he told me of his anguish over the thought that he might try to do this to my oldest sister terrified him. I felt that it didn't matter what someone did to me—that I had no value. This was reinforced when my parents chose not to discuss or address what had happened to me. Thoughts don't always correspond in the body to the abuse it receives, acting out in other ways, both physically and emotionally. Like many who are molested as children, I did not know that I could set boundaries.

When my parents found out about the molestation, they got together with the young man's parents. The abuse stopped. However, it was never discussed again. Unfortunately, the abuse and the betrayal of those who should have been keeping me safe were to shape my future in ways unknown. I learned recently that both my parents had been molested as children and thought this was a typical event, just part of growing up. Approaches toward molestation and abuse have changed over the years, and I know they did the best they could with the information they had.

When I was eleven, I started pulling my hair out, one strand at a time. I was quite a charmer with bald spots. One classmate asked why I did this, and I replied that I didn't know. It wasn't until I was in therapy, decades later, that I understood how it related to depression from the abuse. It has a name now, trichotillomania. Although when I was taken to the doctor as a child, he said I was a nervous child, a daydreamer, and there was no treatment. My dad left our family when I was fourteen. My mother did not have a high school diploma.

She worked at the local theater, selling tickets and went to school to get her GED. This left me with a lot of time on my own. I sought out inappropriate friendships, had risky behaviors, and self-medicated with drugs.

These experiences affected my pregnancies. The inappropriate lessons and reactions of those around me created an environment of distrust of those who would have power over me. I ignored my body's cues that something was going wrong with the pregnancy. My pelvic area was numb to me; I never felt the preterm labor. This numbness continues to trouble me today with the challenges of IBS.

My first baby, Joshua Cody, was born at twenty-eight weeks. My waters released, and I phoned the doctor on call to tell him I was in labor. He told me I couldn't be, it was too early, and I should rest. He was very distracted when I arrived at the hospital an hour later in advanced labor. Upon examination, a nurse told me I was too small. I thought that she meant my hips were too narrow to birth the baby. She told me no, the baby was to be born soon and then left me alone. When I was taken into the labor room, my husband arrived at last. He was frantic to get to me. I could see him through a porthole-shaped window with wild eyes, searching for me. This same awful nurse said, "Why is that gorgeous man with this skinny little girl? He needs a real woman like me."

I felt mortified and totally inadequate. My baby was born, oh so tiny. Joshua Cody lived for twenty-three hours, his prematurity having overcome the neonatal intensive care unit (NICU) efforts. My hospital stay was so devastating. I was put in a room with another mother with a baby in her arms. I cried for hours and stood in the hallway, looking at my baby in an incubator behind the glass wall. I went home with a husband who didn't want to talk about our loss. I tried group therapy at the county clinic and found no one else with the same experience. Our marriage suffered, and my husband died soon after from hemochromatosis.

I married a second time to a wonderful, warm, and caring man. Unfortunately, I went into preterm labor at twenty-six weeks of my second pregnancy. I never felt a thing. The doctor at Stanford University Hospital attempted to stop the labor with magnesium sulfate, a drug used to relax the uterine muscles. Eventually, my waters released, and vaginal exams were continued to assess my progress. I was distraught, scared, confused, and beside myself with stress and guilt. Why was this happening again? I had eaten well and exercised, but I had never resolved the blame, shame, and guilt that followed my childhood abuse and previous birth experience. I developed an infection and fevered at 105 degrees Fahrenheit before an emergency cesarean. Pulmonary edema developed, and I was in the ICU for a week on a respirator. I died as they struggled to get me on the ventilator, and once again, I was revived. Bradley David never took a breath. The devastation of this loss and my shame of not being able to perform as a woman's body was made to do tore my second marriage apart.

After all my doula and hypnosis training, the therapy I had received over the years helped me understand the experiences I had as a child and the patterns that affected my ability to carry a pregnancy to term. It's incredible how the mind-body connection and experiences we had when we were little tended to manifest in physical responses when we are older.

In my third pregnancy, I spent months on bed rest, and my son was born at thirty-four weeks. My daughter was born full-term in my fourth pregnancy after a cerclage at twenty-four weeks and on bed rest for four months. Other than the strict bed rest thing, I loved these pregnancies. These births were quick and easy. Wes spent time in the NICU as he had apnea and bradycardia episodes. My son came home on an apnea monitor. It malfunctioned once, which led to his hospitalization as a precaution. After my training with APPPAH, I learned that my son most likely would not have had these episodes if he had experienced skin-to-skin contact at birth versus being put into an incubator. Studies now show that preemies have better outcomes with skin-to-skin contact versus incubators.

The many tests they ran on him were unnecessary, as it was only a matter of the machine malfunctioning. Why didn't they check that first? And why didn't I think to ask about that possibility? He was very traumatized by all their testing on him, the EKG and X-rays. One doctor with a large batch of interns told me it was okay for my son to cry; it would strengthen his lungs. I pushed him out of the way to pick up Wes and told this inhumane person that he was crying with fear and needed comforting and compassion. The ward nurse applauded my intervention and agreed that the doctor, while accomplished in his field, had only done what he was taught.

Doctors are taught to distance themselves from their patients, block their emotions, and never become emotionally involved. After reading *Kitchen Table Wisdom* by Rachel Noemi Remen, MD, I discovered that this medical care approach is expected. She began as a surgeon, and after much suffering from the consequences of staying emotionally distant from her patients, Dr. Remen developed a medical practice of care for her medical peers. She supports the doctors through therapy, enabling doctors to practice medicine and to care about their patients, connecting with them on an appropriate compassionate level. She teaches them that this philosophy of distancing themselves is harmful to their patients and psyche.

It was glorious to leave the hospital with my daughter within twenty-four hours of her birth. After she was born, I did not hold her for over an hour, as she was passed from the doctor to the nurses for a bath, weighing, and measuring. I begged them to give her to me all the while, and they would only reply, "Just a moment." They were trying to get through their checklist of to-do items, interrupting our essential bonding time.

After my daughter's birth, I started volunteering for Sidelines (www.sidelines.org), an organization to support women with special circumstances during their pregnancies. This was very rewarding and healing for me. I trained volunteers to be peer counselors, visited hospitals to meet women who might want peer counselors, and promoted what we were doing to support these mothers to the doctors and nurses.

Annually, Sidelines had a booth at an obstetrics and gynecological conference to share our services with maternity care providers. A doctor approached me and said with a sneer, "I bet you're pro-choice!" I carefully replied that my role was to support women, no matter their choice. I told him that if abortion were chosen, women would need support, as this is devastating in ways unknown at the time of their decision. If they decided to keep or give the baby up for adoption, they would need support, as they struggled as their lives unfolded. I would never be so arrogant to assume that I would know what might be suitable for someone else. He blinked and walked away. People grow through experiences. Supporting, rather than condemning others for their decisions and gently guiding to virtues and values, will keep our society strong and healthy.

My husband was reassigned to Singapore, so we moved halfway around the world, and I finally found my career passion. In the US, I had worked for decades for IBM and Siemens in administrative management and found myself very bored in Singapore with no career to keep me busy. I was not the type to join the "country club" set and did not enjoy the expat wife's routine of luncheons to discuss how difficult it was to manage their maids. I had researched before I arrived about the differences in the cultures of the US and Singapore, as I did not want to be one of the ugly Americans.

I first volunteered at the Singapore Zoo's Action for Wildlife Corp (AFWC). I was assigned to observe the orangutans in the enclosure—a small cement island—to track the time of and list the activities of a particular orangutan.

Other volunteers were also doing this in situ— in the orangutan's natural environment. The outcome of the hours of observation was that the enclosure was changed, and now the orangutans are free-ranging in the treetops above the visitors within an electrically charged perimeter.

While watching the orangutans one day, I observed that one of the youngsters found a frog at the moat's edge. For twenty minutes, he would pick it up by one leg, smell it, lick it, dangle it, and put it on his head. All the while, the frog played dead. He finally put the frog down; and after a few moments, the frog tried to escape, only to have the youth grab it and start all over with the smelling, licking, etc. Eventually, the young orangutan lost interest in the frog, and it quickly hopped away.

The orangutans usually stayed on their island, not caring for the moat's water; however, a somewhat obese female often waded across the moat and escaped into the crowds, heading for the restaurant nearby. She had been there many times to entertain guests who had paid to have breakfast with an orangutan. She was very tame, and the keeper quickly led her back by her hand to the enclosure.

Once I noticed all the orangutans running to the other side of their island, I watched a number of the keepers running in one direction. I stopped one of the keepers and asked what was going on. He cautioned me to go into the restaurant and not come out until I was told it was safe to do so. Later, we found out that someone had not closed the interior door to the cheetah enclosure, and two had escaped! They were born and raised in the zoo and were quite content to be led back into their enclosure with some food enticement. I did enjoy my time volunteering, but it wasn't filling all my time.

One of the organizers of the AFWC told me of his wife being on bed rest with placenta previa. I offered to call her at the hospital, as it was during the SARS outbreak and no visitors were allowed in the hospital. I called every other day to keep her spirits up, knowing what it is like to be pregnant and on bed rest. This family is still very near and dear to my heart, and we spent many holidays together. She told me about a friend of hers who was taking doula training. I got in touch with the doula in training, which started my path to what I consider my calling.

SECTION 3

The Right Path

Since 2002, I have shed my fear of pregnancy, labor, and birth and have seen many glorious birth experiences. Most of these births were genuinely loving and gentle entries of babies into our world outside the womb. HypnoBirthing (www.hypnobirthing.com) has helped shape my belief systems, and I have found it to significantly impact how women labor and birth. My journey into the birthing field has finally put to rest what happened with my pregnancies—why I have two living children and not four. I have healed myself by learning hypnosis and the power of the mind-body connection. I love teaching parents about all their possibilities for labor and birth and why it is vital to consider the birth their baby would want.

At first, I taught one couple at a time. Those parents told others of their remarkable experiences; and soon, I was teaching five couples, then adding two sessions and building it to ten couples. Before I retired, I had four group classes of five couples each and three private sessions each week. I found them so engaged and eager to learn all their options. I had some amazing couples in my classes, some famous, some who couldn't pay the total price, and some I allowed to attend for free. Unwed mothers in Singapore lose their jobs, and teen mothers have limited support. I found it quite disturbing that the fathers of these babies were still employed. To those young mothers, I provided free classes and free doula support. I believe in supporting our local communities in any way that suits our skills and as time permits.

This spirit of community found its way into my daughter's heart. Part of her two-year high school project found her writing an interactive children's book. She took it to several local schools for children with special needs and to hospitals to read and involve them in the project. KK Women's and Children's Hospital hired her to organize holiday parties and weekly events for hospitalized children. She also encouraged me to foster parent a young baby, Sabrina.

Sabrina was initially to be with us for a few months until her mother could sort her life away from the abusive husband/father. Sabrina came to us at six months old and had already been with two other foster parents. This poor baby did not smile until she was one year old. She had nightmares and challenges napping. Social services eventually moved her to a Mandarin-speaking family at two and a half years old. I fought to keep her in a stable environment or have her adopted into a permanent family. This poor child needed stability, not constant change. Her mother could never break with her husband, even if it endangered Sabrina. I held a going away party for her, trying to instill that change can be a good thing. I invited her new foster family and offered to teach them baby sign language to ease the transition. Unfortunately, they did not attend nor were they interested in learning sign language. She'd be eleven now; I often wonder how she is faring.

THERE WAS A LOT OF LEARNING BUT A LOT OF FUN TOO!

I had one childbirth educator working with me who was so entertaining. She was sitting on a birth ball, talking about the risks of interventions during labor, and the ball shot out from under her. She landed flat on her back with her feet in the air and skirt up to her bum. She was a bit mortified, but I laughed, and I was positive we could charge the parents more for the show!

I instructed parents that the hormone produced during labor was oxytocin, a love hormone, the same one our body generates during lovemaking. Therefore, the same energy that gets the baby in there gets the baby out. So in helping them create their birth plans, I would ask what they needed in their environment for labor to progress smoothly. One dad responded, "Pink fluff and handcuffs." The whole class was rolling on the floor. Ah, these funny, funny parents! His wife went on to have three glorious births.

Another educator came in to share her natural birth story in another class. She had chosen to give birth at home and turned on Dido to aid relaxation. After she had left, one of the dads asked, "Are hospitals okay with didos, and will the vibration hurt the baby?" Everyone was in tears with hysterical mirth, and his wife was slowly shaking her head as I calmly explained that Dido is a singer and he was thinking of a dildo. I added that the vibration of a dildo would not hurt the baby, and they would need privacy in the hospital, so they might want to consider a doula to guard the door.

There were a few that did not enjoy my classes. One mother was from a family of doctors. She complained in my survey that I was dangerous because I encouraged parents to ask their maternity care providers questions to ensure they understood all their options. Another parent was not interested in learning about childbirth and preferred to allow the maternity care provider to direct the entire experience. I think the fact that there were only two detractors of the thousands I taught is a tribute to the parents who seek information to enable them to make informed choices.

I loved ParentLink, the company I owned in Singapore. All we were doing was supporting women in educating themselves about all their birth options and providing the information to allow them to make their desires known. We offered so many services and classes for parents and professionals. I built a community of networking with professionals to provide all the support options I could for the parents who came to us.

For parents, we provided the following:

Fertility hypnosis
Birth hypnosis classes
Planning a pregnancy workshop
ParentLink signature childbirth classes
Newborn care and breastfeeding classes
Infant massage classes
Baby sign language classes
First-aid classes
Pregnancy yoga
Conscious parenting classes
Pre- and postnatal massage
Doula support
Breastfeeding support
Conscious parenting classes
Newly and nearly born gatherings
Complimentary informational talks
Lending library
Water birth tub sales

Organic baby care products cloth nappies
Birth balls
Head massagers
And for professionals, we provided the following:
HypnoBirthing certification
Water birth safely for maternity care providers
Postnatal massage and jamu wrap
Infant massage certification
Dunstan Baby Language certification

I recall attending a water birth and requesting the nurse not to try to lift the baby's head out of the water before it was out of the mother's body. The doctor arrived, grabbed the baby's head, twisted it, and yanked the baby out. I thought so much for a gentle birth. I also realized that someone needed to train the staff about water birth before something went wrong, and they blame the water when it would be their uninformed approach toward birth.

Over the next year, I worked on many different options for the training. Eventually, I was able to corral three midwives to create a workshop for maternity care providers in Singapore and Malaysia. I had four doctors from Indonesia attend one of the workshops conducted in Singapore. As we watched a water birth video, they were chatting in Bahasa among themselves quite animatedly. I asked what they were discussing, and apparently, they had never seen birth other than in the lithotomy position and were quite fascinated. I wondered if they would be willing to attend births in the position of the mother's choice, and they replied, "Yes!" We discussed the importance of positioning and how it can facilitate a more comfortable birth experience. I added to the class the *Birth Move*Ment* video quickly.

I had so much fun building ParentLink up to connect with parents and provide them with all the alternative resources I could find. I had agreements with other like-minded organizations to offer discounts to parents, and I would reciprocate with their clientele.

I took many courses when I owned ParentLink to further my knowledge to support our parents to the best of my abilities. I met so many excellent educators, doulas, parents, and so many more; I cannot even begin to thank them for the blessings I had to meet them, learn from them, support them, and have the ability to bask in the beauty of birth. I taught thousands of parents the opportunities to have joyous birthing experiences for themselves and their babies.

I traveled all around Asia, conducting certification courses. I've taught hundreds of professionals how to teach or utilize the HypnoBirthing philosophy and techniques in their practices, attend water births safely, and the benefits of Dunstan Baby Language. (It's not really a language but an understanding of infants' cries relating to their physical needs.)

I organized a natural birth conference held at National University Hospital for two days. We had a great turnout and many unique speakers covering topics from water births to Dunstan Baby Language and everything in between. Speakers from Australia to the USA traveled to share their knowledge with Singapore professionals and parents.

I was privileged to have Elena Tonetti conduct her rebirthing workshop, and this lovely woman stayed with me for a week. I showed her all around Singapore and all it has to offer. She shared her stories from Russia and the making of her film, *Birth as We Know It*. This is one of my favorite birth films, and I shared it with my parents at my movie nights with popcorn. The film showcases women birthing in the Black Sea with midwives. The midwives and pregnant couples would travel to a remote beach for the summer and give birth in the sea. After viewing the film, a nurse asked Elena how they monitored the women birthing in the Black Sea. Her reply was they didn't. The next question asked was, How did they know the women and babies were okay? She answered that they didn't. I intervened and asked Elena how many babies were born at the birth camps. She responded that over ten years, there were approximately one thousand. I then asked how many losses or complications they had. None. Absolutely zero. I asked Elena how they had such fantastic outcomes. Only healthy women and babies were allowed to birth at the birth camps. All had to attend her rebirthing workshops to eliminate their fear of birthing to remove the trauma from their own birth experience. After attending her rebirthing workshop, I could easily understand their successes. The course eliminated all fears about childbirth, starting with the original introduction to what childbirth is all about, our own birth.

Let me share some lovely birth stories shared by the women I "doulaed" for and from those mothers who shared their stories with me—the ones the doctors at the conference I attended weren't interested in hearing.

SECTION 4

Birth Stories

~Instructions for attending a normal birth~

Watch me.

Watch me lean over and groan.

Watch me sway or rock or dance.

Watch me find my rhythm.

Watch me breathe through a contraction.

As it ends, watch me have a drink of water.

Then watch me relax myself, resting, waiting for the next wave.

Then watch me breathe again.

As you sit there, just outside the vortex, know that my world has shrunk to a bubble.

Be careful. Don't burst it.

A careless word, a bright light…they would be unwelcome right now.

Watch in awe as I play out the age-old miracle.

The world turns for me, the edges go fuzzy, time turns inside out.

There's a big slithery feeling.

And then there's a BABY!

Warm and slippery and fresh from my own body.

Worth every push, grunt, drop of sweat.

Worth every tightening, every stretch mark.

Wait! I'm still in my bubble. It is not finished yet.

Keep your hats and your clamps and your scissors and needles.

Keep your telephones, your scales, your exclamations.

Keep us warm and keep the room quiet and still.

Watch me meet my baby.

Watch his eyes find mine.

Watch his hands and then his mouth find my nipple.

Watch me discover in wonder each finger, each hair, each wrinkle.

Don't disturb the awe of this first meeting.

Please. Just watch. (Samantha Norman)

PREPARATION IS THE KEY

To prepare for my birth with Evita I did many things. One of them that I'm the most grateful for was the community I had both in Singapore and Australia. In Singapore I met with the ParentLink moms from week nine until long after postpartum. Many lovely like-minded ladies who allowed me to hear their stories and ask my questions was really important. I knew since before I was pregnant I wanted a home birth, not sure why since I don't know anyone who had done it in Sweden or the UK where I previously lived, but I was sure to my bones. Still I had questions and fears as any woman hearing successful birth stories finds soothing. I even got to watch one of my friends' videos of her daughter crowning and being born. Somehow it looked easy and made me feel I can do it too.

The group in Australia was my Biodanza-school group. I went once a month to dance and remembered the heightened sensations, flowing hormones, many goosebumps, and intense gratitude for life. Dancing truly helped to ground me and made me feel like a goddess. I was so proud of my curves, being most comfortable in bikini or naked at home. A truly awesome feeling for a woman.

I also did prenatal yoga once a week, had many massages, and really took good care of myself.

With exception for the first trimester when I lived on crisps and fruit, I changed my whole diet to organic and replaced all upmarket creams for olive oil.

We did perineum massage from about week 34-35 regularly, I took supplements, attended the Hypnobirthing course, and listened to the birthing affirmations CD from Hypnobirthing every night. My husband recorded the balloon ride script so I could listen to his soothing voice whilst traveling.

I was very lucky to have a healthy and happy pregnancy. Of course, it wasn't perfect, but it was indeed very good.

Also, choosing my birth team was comforting, and getting to know them in advance was a huge advantage.

My mind was also set on a natural healthy home birth and a healthy child. I made a vision board that I looked at every day. (Ann Sofie)

I felt very blessed to have attended this lovely birth. Ann Sofie and her husband were very much in tune with the baby within, and it was apparent they felt much love for each other.

We had a blessingway ceremony during her ninth month, and among the attendees was another very pregnant mom. We painted a mandala on her baby bump, provided affirmations to help her through her labor, and danced to Psy's "Gangnam Style"—very entertaining with a huge baby bump!

Ann Sofie and her husband had created a vision board on their bedroom door with all they envisioned for this gentle birth.

Dr. Lai Fon Min was the only doctor in Singapore who would attend home births, and he arrived towards the end of Ann Sofie's labor and received this wee one as she sat on a birthing stool just next to the birthing pool.

STORIES OF THE "FIRST HOUR"

I requested skin-to-skin with baby, undisturbed and left in peace, for at least an hour after birth. I had the baby plonked on my chest for just a minute, then he was whisked away for measurements, cleaned up to be checked by the paediatrician. He wouldn't stop crying, so they surmised that he was cold and took him to NICU to be placed under a warming lamp for an hour. I only got him back after more than 2 hours after his birth, even though my husband kept asking for him to be brought back the moment one hour was up. I wish I had insisted on just carrying him. My newborn should have been warmed by my body instead of a lamp. (Goh Hue Yi, Malaysia)

My baby was placed on me immediately after birth with cords and all, but she wasn't moving nor crying, so I was too afraid to hold her, didn't know what I was supposed to do. Then the nurse picked her up, sucked mucus from her nose, and she started to cry. After that, they wrapped her and put her on the warmer. Wished they'd let me hold her, but I didn't know it was the right thing to do, being a first-time mom. Wished they had offered to take pics for us immediately because I regretted not having a pic with baby right after birth. Hubby was all shaken seeing the blood and to think of taking perfect moment pics. Lol. Dr. invited him to cut the cord, though. (Sulastri M. Thamrin, Malaysia)

"Give me my baby! Let me fall in with her first in that magical first hour! To hell with the paed who insisted that she be 'monitored' (more like being held hostage) in the nursery for hours even when she was without any complications! Do not sabotage my breastfeeding by feeding her formula without my consent." I didn't say anything to them. I guess I was too ecstatic to be able to hold my baby for the first time seven hours after I gave birth to her! Ecstatic and sad at the same time. I guess my experience is a hidden blessing. W/out it, I don't think I'd be this passionate about being an advocate of both gentle birth and breastfeeding. I don't want anyone to go through what I went through. Furthermore, had I attempted breastfeeding there 'n then, I might have succumbed to the, "You can't breastfeed because you have inverted nipples" reason that I most likely will get from the nurses, etc. and being a new mom, I know I'm at my vulnerable point. (Chris Anthony, Malaysia)

These stories are so similar to my experience with my daughter. The staff are so engrossed with their protocols or trying to get to the next task that they don't honor the mother-baby dyad. Studies show how important this bonding time is for success in breastfeeding, regulating the baby's temperature, heart, and respiration rate. We now know the importance of the baby's first experience; the baby needs to be treated with respect and acknowledged that they are aware of the experience, and it's their first experience outside the womb! It was warm and wet, and sounds were muted inside the womb. Gently easing them into the outside world, dimming the lights, warming up the room, speaking quietly, and having calming aromatherapy will aid in diminishing the abrupt change in environment.

EXPERIENCES AND LESSONS

Authors' conclusions:

On the basis of women's preferences, vaginal examination seems to be preferred to rectal examination. For all other outcomes, we found no evidence to support or reject the use of routine vaginal examinations in labour to improve outcomes for women and babies. The two studies included in the review were both small, and carried out in high-income countries in the 1990s. It is surprising that there is such a widespread use of this intervention without good evidence of its effectiveness, particularly considering the sensitivity of the procedure for the women receiving it and the potential for adverse consequences in some settings.

The effectiveness of the use and timing of routine vaginal examinations in labour, and other ways of assessing progress in labour, including maternal behavioral cues, should be the focus of new research as a matter of urgency. Women's views of ways of assessing labour progress should be given high priority in any future research in this area. (Cochrane Database CD010088)

My water bag burst at 38 weeks without contractions. Was having birth show as well so I was induced when I was admitted to the hospital at 1.30am. At 9am I was only 3cm dilated so the

gynae ordered drip to induce. I declined epidural because I wanted my 1st birth to be as natural as possible. Wasn't strapped to CTG machine as requested. Nurses were very encouraging and offered me birth ball, reminded me about various positions to ease contractions and a small hand ball to squeeze. At 2pm was checked, but I was only 4cm dilated even though I was already exhausted and distressed. Nobody pushed me for epidural, but I requested it as I was too tired and couldn't stand the pain. My boy was finally delivered close to 8pm after 18 hours. Had 1-hour skin-to-skin after my son was cleaned and weighed. Room-in throughout the hospital stay.

My mum was very upset that my gynae did not do anything to speed up my labour. A Taiwanese colleague told me should it happened in Taiwan, I would have been operated on. I, for one, never doubted my gynae. Read later that as long as baby was not showing signs of distress, they can take their time to be born. Although my boy did have some minor infection, I was injected with antibiotic as my water bag burst too long;. I did not blame my gynae, and I think somehow to a certain degree, I did have some aspects of a gentle birth. (Koh Shir Li, Singapore)

Being tied up to the bed once admitted to the labour ward and I could not move freely is the minus point during labour. I learned my lesson from the first to third births. So, when it came to my fourth, I had told the gynae I don't want epidural, no injection for pain relief, just the laughing gas will do if I need it. The process was faster cause I had very bad ache admit in the morning, my gynae did not put me in labour ward because she know I will dilate slow when I am stressed. So, she moved me to normal ward. Told me to relax, move around more, squat more cause at that time I am around 3.5cm cervix open. But she did remind me if I feel the urge to poo or very painful sharp pain, then she'll get someone to push me to the labour ward. The nurses at normal ward were nice. Checked me hourly. By 6pm I saw blood stain and intense sharp pain again coming at regular timing — that's when I bell the alarm. I walked to labour ward with my hubby because I got no urge to push. I last minute requested for a small towel and warm water shower in the labour ward, then changed clothing. Progress was good, not much pain, dilation had progress also. By 7 plus I was asking for laughing gas due to back pain. 8pm my girl was born. I really enjoyed this labour because it was planned as what I wanted it to be. Very tiring during the pushing, but it was worth it. (Mak Ct, Singapore)

Thanks for allowing us to share, Di. I delivered at TMC twice. I would have liked it if my doctor did not insist on breaking my water bag to augment labour because I totally lost focus after she did that. And I would have much preferred if I wasn't offered VEs every hour or so. Both my labour ended in 2 C sections and I wasn't assisted to do immediate skin-to-skin and latch on, although I had requested it in my birth plan. For a mom who had her birth turn out not the way she wanted, skin-to-skin and immediate latch was the least I felt my gynae could have helped me with, but of course, she was too busy stitching me up. (Umm Umar, Singapore)

Many parents trust their maternity care providers to have the parents' best interests in mind. While most care providers are well educated in helping mothers and babies through challenging experiences, no one has taught them what to do when everything is going right. I believe there is not one ob-gyn who has watched a woman labor from the beginning through to actual birth.

It's incredible how a doula can help the parents stay on track with their birth plan as they wish. It is the birth companion's (often the father) role to be the keeper of the birth plan, as the mother is overwhelmed with what her body is doing and needs to focus on what her body wants her to do. Many birth companions are not comfortable asking to stick to the birth plan when the staff pushes them to keep to their agenda. The doula can suggest questions to ask of the staff to ensure their schedule is for their convenience or honestly a necessary adjustment from the approved birth plan.

I was at one birth, and the parents were refusing vaginal exams. The doctor called me on my hand phone to ask me to tell them they needed one. When I questioned why, he wanted to know if he had time for a haircut. Another time, the doctor wanted a vaginal exam performed to see if he had enough time for a movie. Seriously?

HYPNOBIRTHING PREPARATION: PERSONAL AND POWER

For many years my view on childbirth was, "not until they invent a big enough test-tube!" I was fearful of the pain I'd go through during labour, and I also have a particular loathing for needles. So much so, that on a tour of the local delivery suite while pregnant with my first, I almost fainted when the midwife started talking about epidurals.

Luckily, I stumbled across a hypnobirthing course, which offered some simple techniques and exercises for relaxation and visualization. Every night before bed I'd listen to my hypnobirthing CD's, though I usually fell asleep before the CD had finished, so I could only hope the information was sinking in on a subliminal level!

By 10 days overdue, I found myself Googling, "world's longest ever pregnancy." There was no sign of this baby making an appearance any time soon! That night we had dinner with friends, and we'd barely got to bed when I felt a "ping" inside my belly at around 1:15am and stood up to a gush of fluid - my waters had gone! I was really surprised as I'd had no surges or other signs of labour. "Try and get some sleep and we'll deal with it in the morning," my husband suggested.

Naturally, baby had other ideas and within a couple of hours I was experiencing regular, powerful surges every 4-5 minutes and the sudden sensation of nausea and shakiness that the hypnobirthing classes had prepared me for. Around 4am, as I was sipping a cup of chamomile tea, my doula, Jennie, arrived. My husband scurried around gathering the hospital bags while I lay on the bed focusing on my relaxation techniques.

Shortly after 5am we arrived at hospital and to my frustration, the surges seemed to slow down massively. I'd been warned that this often happens – and what probably didn't help was a rather uncomfortable internal examination which showed I was already 8cm open. Later on, the doctor wanted to do another internal examination, but I broke out of my trance to shout, "no more exams until Biswas [my obstetrician] gets here!" I felt incredibly nauseous and was suffering an attack of the hiccups after every surge. If I wasn't in labour, I'd have laughed at this!

I lay on my side listening to the affirmations and relaxation script on the hypnobirthing CD. My other most essential piece of birthing equipment was a cool, wet flannel placed over my eyes, which was my way of blocking out all the distractions going on around me. Jennie told me I had a lot of tension in my jaw, so I focused on relaxing my jaw with each surge by letting out a low "ahhh" sound. Such a simple thing, but it really helped to get things moving again.

By 6am I noticed my breathing had started to change and I could sense things were getting closer. I spent some time sitting on the toilet and then the birthing stool, but eventually I just wanted to lie on the bed. Biswas, my obstetrician, showed up at 8:30am and wanted to move me onto my back to deliver the baby. "No thanks, I'll stay on my side and you can just lift up my leg," I retorted. And with that, just before 9am, baby Abigail was born. It was an incredibly calm delivery, and she went straight onto my belly and started to breastfeed shortly afterwards.

My second delivery was even quicker. In truth, I'd not practiced the hypnobirthing routines as thoroughly as I had with my first, but like riding a bike, it all came back to me in the moment. My labour started around 4am with powerful surges every few minutes – and a sudden urge to use the bathroom showed me that things were well underway!

I went to the spare bedroom so I could focus on my relaxation techniques – and also to avoid disturbing my husband and Abigail (who'd sneaked into our bed during the night). By around 6am though, I could sense the baby was coming soon, so it was off to hospital.

This time around I was not prepared to have any internal examinations, much to my midwife's chagrin. I could tell things were progressing anyway, and I had my trusty cool wet flannel and remembered to relax my jaw and do my "ahhh's."

The labour felt much more intense this time. I asked for gas and air, but quickly abandoned it as my throat felt really dry and waves of nausea washed over me. After a short while, I could literally feel my breathing change and noticed my body was bearing down. "The baby's coming!" I told the midwife. "Nonsense," she said. "You wouldn't be talking to me like this if the baby was

coming." Reluctantly, I let her examine me. I was fully open.

My doula suggested I let gravity help by kneeling on the bed and leaning over the back of the bed in an upright position. Professor Biswas, my obstetrician, appeared briefly by my side and we had a quick chat—of which I remember absolutely nothing as I was focusing so intently on my labour and breathing. "I'll see you later," Biswas said, gathering up his notes. He was obviously not expecting much action for a while.

As Biswas left the room, I was hit with an adrenaline rush—an incredible wave of nausea and heat. I didn't know whether to throw up or strip off all my clothes first. A nurse shot out of the room and yelled down the corridor, "Prof—come back!" and literally within the next surge, the baby's head was out. It was nearly 9am when Georgina was born, pretty much the same time as her sister was born three years earlier. (Rachael Herring)

Preparing mentally as well as physically is necessary for a gentler, more comfortable birth experience. I loved teaching childbirth classes and miss it now that I'm retired. Rachael worked hard to prepare for her births and was committed to her vision of birth. Her husband vocally reinforced their approved vision of birth by ordering an intern out who was flicking on lights and demanding to do internal exams.

Mickey Mongan used to encourage the HypnoBirthing educators to have a stuffed toy gorilla. The male gorilla stands guard over the female when she is in labor. He knows that if left alone and feeling safe, she can birth his progeny. Have to love the HypnoBirthing birthing companions standing guard, keeping the birth moving along as planned.

BROKEN WATERS AND RESPECT

Amniotomy for shortening spontaneous labour
Rebecca MD Smyth
Carolyn Markham
Therese Dowswell
Editorial Group: Cochrane Pregnancy and Childbirth Group
Published Online: 18 JUN 2013
Assessed as up-to-date: 10 JUN 2013
DOI: 10.1002/14651858.CD006167.pub4
Copyright © 2013 The Cochrane Collaboration. Published by John Wiley & Sons, Ltd.
From google scholar http://onlinelibrary.wiley.com/doi/10.1002/14651858.CD006167.pub4/abstract

Evidence does not support routinely breaking the waters for women in normally progressing spontaneous labour or where labours have become prolonged.

The aim of breaking the waters (also known as artificial rupture of the membranes [ARM], or amniotomy); is to speed up and strengthen contractions, and thus shorten the length of labour. The membranes are punctured with a crochet-like long-handled hook during a vaginal examination, and the amniotic fluid floods out. Rupturing the membranes is thought to release chemicals and hormones that stimulate contractions. Amniotomy has been standard practice in recent years in many countries around the world. In some centres it is advocated and performed routinely in all women, and in many centres it is used for women whose labours have become prolonged. However, there is little evidence that a shorter labour has benefits for the mother or the baby. There are a number of potential important but rare risks associated with amniotomy, including problems with the umbilical cord or the baby's heart rate.

The review of studies assessed the use of amniotomy in all labours that started spontaneously. There were 15 studies identified, involving 5583 women, none of which assessed whether amniotomy increased women's pain in labour. The evidence showed no shortening of the length of first stage of labour and a possible increase in caesarean section. Routine amniotomy is not recommended as part of standard labour management and care. (Smyth et al., *Amniotomy for shortening spontaneous labour*)

Thanks for asking—I would have preferred if she had asked me if I wanted my water bag burst first instead of just saying, "We're going to have to burst your water bag now..." and went ahead to do it. And all I remember after that was a gush of warm fluid, the bed soaked with it all, and sudden excruciating contractions which I couldn't even try to control with my breathing. After baby came out, followed by the placenta, there was just so much blood it felt like a state of shock more than happiness, and they went on their merry way to clean baby up without me having even had the chance to hold him yet. I would also have preferred like someone mentioned above, if they weren't so persistent on offering pain relief like epidural (had to honestly scream "no" at one point)—I feel it just adds to the stress and pressure. (Tish Corvinus, Malaysia)

My gynae broke my water bag, inserted the drip "to hasten labour," and gave me an episiotomy—all before I could say anything. Being first time parents, both hubby 'n' I did not have the guts to tell her we wanted otherwise (partly because everybody in the labour ward made it seem like the baby was in danger 'n' had to come out fast). We felt like we were in a factory line of baby production because we were constantly being hurried. My husband was surprised at how the midwives kept harping on the fact that I didn't opt for epidural—they made it seem like taking an epidural was the norm and the way to go. (Mia Maya, Malaysia)

Even though studies show that these procedures are unnecessary, what stands out the most is the lack of respect for the mother. How is it possible to perform an amniotomy without her consent?

I discussed one long labor with the labor ward nurse. I mentioned that the doctor was lovely for not trying to speed up the labor as long as the mother and baby were doing fine. The nurse had the most dismayed look on her face. I asked with which doctors she liked to work. The reply was the doctors who speed labor up and the mothers who use epidurals. This discussion was a huge epiphany for me. That is what she was trained to do. It was within her comfort zone. She knew how to support women with an epidural. Supporting women through a natural birth was not her cup of tea, as she didn't know what to do to help those mothers. She was uncomfortable supporting them. I offered to the ward head nurse to provide training, but somehow it never happened.

EPIDURAL AND CHOICE: A POWER STRUGGLE

> Thanks for asking, Di...I would have appreciated it if they would stop asking if we want epidural repeatedly and that its better we take it before it's too late...I was having bearable pain during my first birth and did not need any epidural...But I still took it because they kept asking repeatedly and I felt very pressured to do so...Now that I know better, aiming for a natural birth this time around. (Nurbee Selamat, Malaysia)

Having a birth plan can make a huge difference in how the staff interacts with parents. Having the birth companion supporting the mother is paramount to having the birth experience that the mother and baby will enjoy.

And again, respect! If a mother has requested not to be offered an epidural, why keep repeating? I do believe that it is what the staff is most comfortable with. They know how to support women with an epidural.

ONE BABY, TWO PERSPECTIVES

I include below a birth story from the mom's perspective and from her doula. This mother used the HypnoBirthing techniques learned in class. This doctor is the first to be open to supporting women wanting natural births in Singapore. The hospital was open to women's birth plans as well.

Isabel's birth story
November 30 2006, Thursday
November 30, 2:00 a.m.

> Woke up with contractions, thought they were practice contractions because they were irregular and passed after about four contractions. There were no other signs: no show, no water bag breaking. Went back to sleep.

November 30, 4:00 a.m.

> This time woke up with stronger contractions. Had to stand and lean against the cot next to my bed to cope with the contractions. Walked and breathed through the contractions. Laying down made the pain worse.

November 30, 4:30 a.m.

Woke Kiat up. Had to prod him quite a few times before he woke up, he was deep asleep in la-la-land. Asked him to time my contractions first before we decide to call our doula and mom. Contractions were about 60 secs–75 secs each time. This meant that I was in advance labour. Found it a bit hard to believe it.

Called Mairead, our stand-by doula, to inform her about the contractions and that we will call her later if we were heading to the hospital.

Had to stand and hug Kiat each time the contractions came. I was listening to the hypno-birthing CD, but it was hard to concentrate. I got a bit irritated when I needed his help with the contractions and he had to go to the toilet, blow his nose, gel his hair, etc. Good thing I had packed our hospital bag and left in our car already, but still had to remind him to bring some important stuff with us.

November 30, 5:30 a.m.

Called mom to come over and look after Joshua. Called Mairead to meet us at the hospital.

November 30, 5:45 a.m.

Mom came over and first thing she did was ~~to~~ brush her teeth!

We headed out and I walked really slowly as the contractions were coming fast and furious. Remembered it was a cool and peaceful pre-dawn hour and I was appreciative of the tranquility as we made our way to the car.

In the car, listened to hypnobirthing CD, and it helped to listen to affirmations of a calm and joyous birth that we were hoping to have.

November 30, 6:00 a.m.

Reached Thomson Medical. Kiat had to park the car, although I wanted him to just park in the doctor's lot as I had a contraction just then and needed his support. Had to lean against the pillar in the lobby. The attendant asked if I needed a wheelchair. Sitting or lying down only made the pain worse.

Mairead was already there and Kiat soon joined us. We took the lift to the labour wards, and it was my first time seeing the place even though I had been here before when I delivered Joshua. My eyes were half closed then. This time, I seemed to be stronger and calmer. I could even tell the nurse that I didn't want the birthing pool. I had to stop halfway in the corridor to lean on Kiat and breath through the contraction. It seemed to take forever to walk to the labour room.

When I reached the labour room, the nurse wanted me to lie down for an external monitoring, but told her I would like it done standing. Kiat also firmly repeated my preference. She tried to persuade me to lie down because she said that the reading will be more accurate and it will be easier to read. Yeah, but it's not easy for me to lie down. Only makes the pain worse. Insisted on standing and she strapped the external monitor on me. The monitoring was a hindrance as I was experiencing stronger contractions. I asked how soon the monitor could come off. Thankfully, the reading was clear and Isabel's heart beat was good. Next, the nurse asked me to lie down for a vaginal examination, and I was getting quite tired with this nurse. She said she needed to know how dilated I was in order to decide whether to call Dr. Tseng to come in. It was really painful to be on the bed.

I was 8cm dilated. I was really surprised because before coming into the hospital, I was wondering if I made the correct choice coming in because what if I was not dilated enough and there will be more interventions which I didn't want. I didn't imagine everything to be happening so soon. But I was thankful that the end was very near in sight.

After I got off the bed, I had to kneel because I felt the urge to bear down. I already decided that I was not going to be on the bed this time. Kneeling on the pillows with my head propped on the bed was one of the possible birthing positions I planned to be in, and it was so natural to slide down from the bed after the vaginal examination to the kneeling position.

Mairead helped to ease the pain with her massage on my back. It was really good to have the massage and smell the lavender oil. She was also affirming me on how good I was doing. She was also very respectful of our need for a peaceful birth and spoke in a soft voice.

I practiced my breathing and when I felt the urge to bear down, I remembered to breathe down from my chest and I opened up my legs each time giving more space for baby to come through. I was feeling tired, but I told myself to give it my all. I just let go off my voice each time I beared down. Felt something slid out but it was only meconium. I knew I had to bear down more and opened up my legs while still kneeling. Dr. Tseng said he could see the head, and I felt my perineum stretching. Kiat asked if he could catch baby, and Dr. Tseng told him how to.

November 30, 7:20 a.m.

I gave it my all and birthed Isabel Sng Min En! When I heard her cry as she came out, I was so happy I cried. It was wonderful to birth Isabel this way.

I rested on the bed and latched Isabel to me. She was really good at latching and sucking. Her eyes were open and she looked really alert. She looked very different from Joshua. I reminded myself that I should not compare the two, just value each of their special traits.

I held her for a long time before she was measured, and Kiat was with her for the measurement. She weighed 3.26kg, 51cm in length and 34cm for head circumference. I also held her for the Vit K injection and told her that it will sting but it will be over soon. Could hear her scream out loud. She has really powerful lungs!

I am really glad that the birth went so smoothly, it was the calm and joyous birth we envisioned.

And the doula's version:

Mairead's phone rings. It's Silas. Baby Isabel must be on her way!

"Hi Mairead. Sharon is in labour. Her contractions are lasting quite long."

I asked whether Sharon and Silas would like me to come to their house or meet them at the hospital.

"Let me check with Sharon. I will call you back shortly," Silas replied.

Mairead hopped out of bed and had a quick shower to wake herself up.

05:30 a.m.

Mairead was just dressed when Silas called back. "The contractions are lasting quite long. We will meet you at Thomson."

"Okay. I am on my way," Mairead replies. She calls a taxi and grabs a quick slice of toast and glass of water while she waits for it to arrive.

06:00 a.m.

Mairead arrives at Thomson Medical Centre at the same time as Silas and Sharon. Mairead can see that Sharon is already in advanced labour. She is walking very slowly and deliberately and is very inwardly focused. A couple of steps inside Thomson, Sharon stops for a surge. She turns to Silas and leans into him for support. She breathes her way through the surge beautifully. Once the surge has passed, Silas checks with Sharon whether it is okay for him to leave to park the car. Mairead accompanies Sharon up to the Delivery ward in the lift.

06:05 a.m.

Mairead and Sharon are greeted at the Delivery suite by Nurse Susan Lim. She shows us to Room 8. Silas arrives. Sharon immediately settles into an upright labouring position at the far side of the bed. She stands with her legs apart and leans onto the bed for support.

Nurse Susan would like to monitor the baby. "Would Sharon please lie on the bed?" she enquires.

"No, my wife would rather stand," Silas replied.

"But it is much harder to attach the monitor when your wife is standing," Nurse Susan replies.

"My wife would rather stand," Silas gently but firmly insists. "It is written in our birth plan."

Throughout the labour and after the birth, Silas remains a steadfast guardian of Sharon's birthing environment and their birth plan.

"Okay. Let's see if we can attach the monitor while you are standing," Nurse Susan concedes.

06:07 a.m.

Within a minute the monitor is attached and the rhythmic sound of Isabel's strong and steady heartbeat fills the air. Silas rubs Sharon's back while Mairead prepares the birthing environment. The lights are dimmed and the hypnobirthing cd is played. At Sharon's request Mairead heats a rice sock and applies it to her lower back. After Mairead has blown up the birth ball she takes over massaging Sharon's hips and lower back from Silas.

06:27 a.m.

After 20 minutes of monitoring Nurse Susan asks if she can perform a vaginal examination. Sharon and Silas agree. Sharon lies up on the bed and Susan announces that Sharon is at 8cms.

This is great news! Sharon smiles—and so she should. She has made amazing progress and has remained totally calm and focused.

Nurse Susan leaves to inform Dr. Tseng and Sharon quickly moves back into her original labouring position alongside the bed. After another couple of surges Sharon sinks down onto her knees. She asks for a pillow and shuffles around until she is comfortable.

Sharon is starting to show signs of advanced labour. She has firmly anchored into her birthing position and is very inwardly focused. Her head now rests on her arms and her eyes remain closed. She is also feeling hot and cold. On her feet Sharon is wearing a pair of cute candy stripped white ankle socks and she pulls the hood of her navy jacket up over her head.

06:35 a.m.

Mairead notices the first signs of her mucous seal traveling down her leg, so she places a couple of inkpads on the pillow and surrounding ground. Nurse Maryanne brings in one of the foam mats from Room 6. We place it beneath Sharon to afford her some extra padding on her knees. She remains deeply focused and is breathing beautifully. The hypnobirthing CD continues to play in the background, and Mairead is now busy massaging Sharon's hips and sacrum with lavender oil.

06:40 a.m.

There is more mucous seal trickling down Sharon's legs. Silas leaves to fetch a mirror so that he can get a clearer view of baby Isabel's progress. He returns, mirror in hand and crouches down to get a good view of the amazing changes in Sharon's body.

"Look at how beautifully her hips are opening up," Mairead points out.

"Oh yes, I can see that," Silas replies. He is completely mesmerized.

06:45 a.m.

Dr. Tseng arrives in with Nurse Maryanne. Mairead is kneeling behind Sharon, massaging her hips and sacrum and applying quite a bit of counter-pressure now during the peak of her surges. Dr. Tseng observes for a couple of minutes and is then happy to leave Sharon and Silas to labour for a bit longer on their own. Nurse Maryanne tells Silas to press the red button when we require further assistance.

06:50 a.m.

Sharon and Silas are making fantastic progress. Sharon has started to feel the urge to bear down and has begun to make a low grunting sound at the peak of her surges. She is rocking her hips now and pushing right back into Mairead's hands during surges.

"Do you feel like you want to push?" Silas asks Sharon. She nods in reply.

07:00 a.m.

Silas continues to observe Sharon's progress in the mirror. After two long powerful contractions and some more vocalization from Sharon, Silas decides that it is time to call in Dr. Tseng. He leaves the room and returns within a couple of minutes followed by Dr. Tseng and Nurse Maryanne. Dr. Tseng suits up and kneels behind Sharon. Silas passes him the mirror. Mairead moves to one side and continues to offer massage.

07:07 a.m.

Sharon's waters break. There is meconium present.

"Okay Sharon, start pushing hard with your contractions," urges Dr. Tseng. "The baby should descend very quickly now."

Sharon remarks that her knees are slipping off the pillow. She shifts slightly in an effort to regain a steady grounding. Along comes a powerful surge. Sharon is vocalizing well. The pitch in her voice has risen slightly. Her perineum is starting to bulge. As the surge passes, she again comments that her knees are slipping. Silas and Mairead place a foot against either knee to give Sharon the support she needs. Mairead continues to massage. Nurse Maryanne urges Sharon to push hard with her next contraction.

07:10 a.m.

Another powerful surge. Isabel is beginning to crown.

"She's coming Sharon, I can see her head." Silas updates Sharon on what is happening.

Sharon takes a rest between surges.

Silas seeks advice from Dr. Tseng on where to position himself to receive baby Isabel and then moves into place. He holds his hands out, calm and steady, to receive his daughter.

"Your body is opening up wonderfully. During the next surge, breathe right down to your baby. Isabel is almost here," Mairead whispers to Sharon.

Sharon breathes much deeper with her next surge, the pitch of her vocalization lowers and her perineum stretches beautifully. We can see more of baby Isabel's head.

Sharon steadies herself for her next surge. This could be the one! Baby Isabel's head remains clearly visible between surges.

"That was fantastic Sharon. Just do that again. Breathe right down to your baby," Mairead again encourages.

Baby Isabel's head emerges with the next surge.

"There's her head," says Dr. Tseng.

"She's coming Sharon, I can see her head," says Silas without taking his eyes off Isabel. He sits poised to catch baby Isabel with the next surge.

"I can see her head, Sharon, she is so beautiful," says Mairead.

07:20 a.m.

Baby Isabel is born with the next surge. She gives a little cry and is quickly passed to Sharon. Sharon sits back on her heels to gently cradle her beautiful new baby daughter. Silas stands proudly by, smiling from ear to ear. After a quick cuddle, baby Isabel is passed back to Silas while Nurse Maryanne and Mairead help Sharon onto the bed.

07:25 a.m.

Isabel is suctioned to remove any meconium from her airways. Sharon removes her top. She is keen to cuddle her baby and initiate breastfeeding. After a minute Sharon asks that her baby be returned. Isabel is quickly swaddled in an orange blanket and returned to Mommy, who offers her breast.

"I think she looks like you," Sharon says to Silas.

"She doesn't have any dimples," Sharon remarks.

07:35 a.m.

Sharon's placenta is delivered. Isabel is now latched on and suckling happily and Dr. Tseng informs Sharon that her perineum is intact. Wow. What an amazing woman!

07:40 a.m.

Mairead leaves Sharon, Silas and Isabel to spend some time together alone.

07:55 a.m.

Mairead returns with a coffee for Silas and refills Sharon's water bottle. Isabel is still suckling happily. Silas is busy taking photos and admiring his new daughter.

08:06 a.m.

Nurse Anne arrives to administer Isabel's vitamin K injection. Sharon cradles Isabel in her arms and quietly explains to her what is going to happen and reassures her that everything will be okay. Isabel cries briefly after her injection, but soon settles again on Mommy's breast.

"She cries much louder than Joshua did," Silas remarks.

"Yes, she does," Sharon agrees.

08:20 a.m.

Isabel startles a couple of times at the strange sounds and voices of her new environment. Sharon and Silas both remark that Isabel is sensitive to sound just like her big brother Joshua was when he was born.

08:25 a.m.

Silas tears himself away from Sharon and Isabel to take care of the paperwork. Mairead keeps them company until he returns about 10 minutes later. When Silas returns he takes some more photos and Mairead gets her first cuddle.

"Would you like to hold baby Isabel Mairead?" he asks.

"Yes, of course," Mairead had been patiently waiting her turn to cuddle the gorgeous Isabel!

08:45 a.m.

There is a bit of confusion over room availability so Mairead decides to stick around until Sharon and Isabel are comfortably resettled on the postnatal ward.

09:15 a.m.

Mairead finally says goodbye to Sharon and Silas and Isabel. They have been temporarily accommodated in a shared room until a single room becomes available later that afternoon.

Mairead leaves the hospital with a spring in her step. What a lovely start to the day!

Congratulations Sharon and Silas

It's lovely to compare the two stories to see the differences and what is the same. Both had a positive perspective on the experience!

CONFLICT OF INTEREST AND CHANGING PLANS

The art of vaginal breech birth at term on all fours

Hajo I. J. Wildschut, Hinke van Belzen-Slappendel, and Suze Jans

Author information ▶ Article notes ▶ Copyright and license information ▶

Go to the following:

Key clinical message

> Despite a shift in clinical practice favouring cesarean section for breech presentation, adequate skills are still needed for a safe vaginal breech birth. This case report illustrates the physiological mechanism of vaginal breech birth. (Wildschut et al., *The art of vaginal breech birth at term on all fours*)

Had a "war" with my first gynae as she kept saying my firstborn was too big and that I wouldn't be able to give birth if I went overdue, which I did. That was not without pressure from her who insisted I go for a CTG every other day in return for not taking up her offer for an induction. When I finally had my mucus plug dislodged, instead of waiting for labour to progress naturally again, she insisted I come in the morning after to have an induction. I was so upset but my water bag burst that night itself with stained liquor, so I panicked and went into labour. But yes, like the sisters above, I was already prepped for a C section because no food was allowed and not even water. However due to the meconium, I was forced to stay in bed strapped on w the ctg. When doc came in the next day, she was quite sneaky I felt. She kept saying "well, you're already 5cm dilated and we can just wait another 5 hrs. But look, your baby's heartbeat keeps dipping." That just freaked me and hubby out. When I asked the midwives if I cud walk since gravity cud help, they laughed at me and got angry when hubby insisted we give it a try. Since baby was just struggling, we gave in to an emergency C section and not even the half-body one. Seriously disappointing...hoping for a better birth experience w no 2 and I have changed gynae...Phew (Nabila Hanim, Malaysia)

I would like doctors to be more open to vaginal delivery for breech babies. My doctor laughed off ECV, and I felt stupid going through the idea with her, and pushed me to elect for C-sect at 38 weeks. She also waved off the idea to delay clamping my baby's cord—she claims there is no good evidence to back that up. Not sure whether I was crazy enough to believe what I found online and that she is more in the know, OR that she is sorely outdated and I should have been more assertive... how do you tell what is her agenda? (Abdullah Khan, Singapore)

Saying "No" to Induction
Judith A. Lothian, PhD, RN, LCCE, FACCE
Author information ▶ Copyright and License information ▶
Go to the following:

> Abstract Induction rates have increased dramatically. A childbirth educator wonders how she can help pregnant women say "no" to induction. This column describes the last days and weeks of pregnancy as vitally important for both the mother and her baby, insuring the baby's maturity and the mother's readiness for labour. Women are encouraged to appreciate the last days and weeks of pregnancy and to have confidence that when a woman's body and her baby are ready, labor will begin spontaneously. This information, as well as knowledge of how induction alters the process of normal labor and birth and increases the possibility of having a near-term infant, is the foundation for informed refusal. (Lothian, *Saying "No" to Induction*)

https://www.ncbi.nlm.nih.gov/pmc/articles/PMC1595289/

> I wished my doctor would have let me wait another two weeks to see if my labour would start itself instead of pressuring me to induce just because I'd hit 40 weeks and she said the baby was big. (Aadilah Affandi)

Choosing the care providers who are on the same page as the parents in their approach to birth is critical in achieving the birth experience you want and expect. The best way to determine if the care provider will support a natural birth is to ask the following open-ended questions:

How do you feel about me laboring and birthing off the bed?

How long are you comfortable for me to labor?

When do you find it necessary to induce labor?

How do you feel about my eating and drinking during labor?

How do you feel about me having a doula at the birth?

What is your cesarean rate?

And if you are still in doubt about your doctor's protocols, seek a second opinion. Find through research which doctors in your area will support natural birth options.

Studies show that the vernix should be left on the baby, as this is a natural bacterial barrier. It also helps with the bonding between mother and baby—and that is not considering the mother's wishes for her baby as discussed and approved in her birth plan.

> I didn't want my baby 'roughed up' in a towel and didn't expect it to happen when I handed her over to be weighed. It was in my birth plan, but they just went with their usual practice. It was awful to watch as a Mum and my daughter hasn't liked the midwife who did it ever since whenever we have seen her…I realize the midwife did it, but lots of doctors do too and there was no reason to do it.
>
> Also, to be able to be on the same ward to sleep when your baby is in neonatal care…distance makes a massive difference and honoring Mums' wishes to not give formula, providing accurate info about baby's tummies and formula—we were allocated really poor info when we were in NICU, which had massive impact. (Wendy Langshaw, Singapore)

THE FULL STORY: BIRTH DOESN'T START AT BIRTH

When I found out that I was pregnant, I wasn't quite ready to accept the news. Well, okay, I wasn't on birth control but we weren't trying either, and considering how many times we do, you know what, the probability of me getting pregnant is really rather low. Not to mention that I only have one ovary left because I had an ovarian cyst when I was 15...

Anyway, I wasn't quite ready for the news, as I just don't know if I'm ever prepared to be a mom. I know I'd like to have kids, just not sure when. I didn't take the news very well as I start to envision my life changing; to a direction where there'll be less and less "me" and more and more of the child. I simply am not that selfless yet. I start to feel a little depressed...On the other hand, David is much more on board with the idea and excited about what's coming.

I was supposed to meet 2 business associates for drinks two days after discovering that I was pregnant. I debated whether I should tell them about it outright, as I was pregnant, which might take me out of the market, and that's not what I wanted. At the same time, what kind of excuse could I make to avoid drinking? They both know that I enjoy my wine and cocktails. I decided to

come clean, and to my surprise, these 2 ladies were overjoyed for me! They opened their heart and told me how much they wanted to have a child and had been trying but still couldn't conceive. I felt like such a dork and looking at them, 2 successful career women longing for a child, and me, carrying one inside me but not appreciating the miracle...That meeting made me realize that this is indeed a blessing and that I should be happy with our baby's arrival.

Although I didn't get into the "mommy" frenzy and buy everything cute in sight, I did purchase a few books about pregnancy and started learning about what to expect. Since I found out about my pregnancy only in the 12th week, I had pretty much skipped the first trimester unknowingly. I could only comfort myself that everything I had done during those first 3 months shouldn't affect the baby that much. After all, I traveled on a 2-month long business trip in India, under great stress and not in the best/cleanest environment. I ate street side food, often drank to de-stress at night, fell sick and took some unknown antibiotics during the trip, I just hoped that nothing I had done would harm the baby inside me now...

After accepting that a new life is on his/her way and that this is meant to be, I knew that I wanted a "painless" way of delivery. Everyone has horror stories, my mom's being the worst. She talked about how painful childbirth was, that her hands were rubbed raw bleeding from hanging onto the metal hospital bed rails. It was such a trauma that after my brother's birth, she had decided not to have any more kids, but I came along as a surprise 14 months later.

I remember watching some 20/20 or 60 Minutes type program back in the States that there's a method of birthing known as HypnoBirthing. The report followed pregnant women into delivery and compared "normal" childbirth and HypnoBirthing. Moms who opted for normal delivery were screaming in pain, while the moms who chose HypnoBirthing simply paced around in the hospital room quietly. "That's what I want to do if I ever have a kid one day," I said to myself.

I was a little worried that HypnoBirthing might not be practiced at all in Singapore. Fortunately, when I Googled it, I found 2 centres in Singapore that offer HypnoBirthing classes, and I immediately emailed one of them—Parentlink.

The first meeting at Parentlink was a screening of the documentary "What Babies Want?" It was interesting. I didn't quite realize that there's such a movement for natural and holistic approach to pregnancy and birthing. Honestly, I'm not really a holistic person, and I am not a strong advocate for natural birth. I just wanted the option of being free to walk around during labor, and I couldn't imagine the pain of putting a needle into my spine if I opted to have epidural. And since I had kind of a caesarean operation when the doctor removed my ovarian cyst when I was 15, I knew that caesarean is a big operation that will take time to recover. Plus, really, if I don't ever feel natural labor, how would I know how much my mom had gone through for me? ;-)

The HypnoBirthing class was actually a perfect choice. It introduced a positive approach to birthing, but it also reminded me to keep a positive outlook on life. It came at a good time as

I was also dealing with some family issues during my pregnancy.

Initially, I worried about not being able to be "hypnotized" or to keep myself in a relaxed state as I am an impatient, anxious control freak! These characteristics serve me well at work, but certainly not as an expecting mom. I actually had asked a friend of mine, "Isn't meditation boring?" when she suggested that I meditate to de-stress! LOL However, after some practicing, I find that the relaxation methods taught in class work well in daily life and that by practicing it often, I just might be able to relax and not think about "pain" during labor.

I listened to the birth affirmation CD (basically it's a CD that reminds you to think positively about labor & birth) almost every day during my train rides to and from work for the last 3 months. I also practiced the breathing techniques taught in class and listened to the relaxation CD at least once a week. David was supposed to practice some relaxation methods with me, but we didn't really do it much. I got a little worried that I hadn't been a good enough student and told myself that we'd "get on it" after I left work on July 31. After all my guess date was August 7, we'd still have one full week to get our act together. ;-)

We also attended the antenatal class at Mount Alvernia and toured the place. Although the hospital and staff seemed fine, I found the hospital bed very repulsive as it's so generic, cold and sterile, and I just couldn't imagine myself lying on that bed with my legs up pushing a baby out. So, I started thinking about having a water birth. Waterbirth always seemed so "natural" for me, after all the baby has been in water for 9 months, coming to the world via water just seems right. I thought more and more about it and finally decided to combine water birth with HypnoBirthing. It took me a while to coordinate with Di at Parentlink as we weren't sure if we could find a birthing pool and a doula in time. The stars finally aligned, Di found a birthing pool and her slot freed up, so she was able to be our doula!

Little did we know that Ariah, who probably inherited the impatient quality from her mom, decided to come early! Less than 24 hours after finalizing our paperwork with Di, Ariah was in my arms.

I left work early on Friday, in a mad rush to the doctor's office as I didn't feel the baby's movement much since the day before. I had a scheduled appointment on Saturday afternoon but called the clinic to see if I could move it up since I felt a little uneasy with the decline in movement. The baby was usually rather active. When the nurse heard that over the phone, she simply said, "You should come now!" I wasn't worried till I listened to that and I left in a hurry.

Dr. Paul Tseng was on leave, so Dr. Phyllis Liauw attended to me. She had me strapped to EFM monitoring and then performed an ultrasound to check on the baby. The baby was indeed a little less active but was doing just fine. Dr. Liauw then advised me to keep a movement chart just to make sure that things were okay, and that I should still see Dr. Tseng the next day.

The baby still didn't move much Friday evening nor Saturday morning, so I went back to the clinic, and Dr. Tseng conducted another

EFM. Again, the baby was asleep but doing okay. Dr. Tseng advised me to continue monitoring the movement and to come back the following week. However, now that I've experienced EFM, I was happy with our decision to go with a waterbirth, I certainly do not want to be strapped on EFM all the time during labor!

We went about the rest of our Saturday as initially planned.

It was a pretty busy day, David and I met up with some friends of mine, a financial planner and finally with Di in the late afternoon for our prenatal consultation. We had a relaxing dinner at Manhattan Fish Market at Central, right across the street from Parentlink, and we decided to go home early to spend some time with our dog Sparky. We felt that he's been neglected with our busy schedule during the week, and although nothing is exciting on TV that night, we were simply happy to be home with him.

We went to bed late, as usual, we are typical night owls. I think it was about 1 AM when we finally hit the sack. I got up at about 3:30 AM to use the bathroom, and I felt mild contractions in my tummy, very similar to menstrual cramps. They weren't really affecting me, and I was able to sleep through them, although I was awakened a few more times as I kept feeling the urge to use the bathroom.

As the night progressed, I felt like pooping more and more, but nothing ever came out when I went to the bathroom. At the same time, the "cramps" felt stronger. I looked at the clock, and it was just about 6 AM. I didn't think I needed to wake David up as I wasn't in pain, and there's nothing he could do at this point, either.

Around 7:30 AM, the surges were noticeably more substantial, so I woke David up and told him, "I think I'm having contractions." We decided to time the surges. I'd tell David, "Okay, it's starting." He'd count "1 thousand, 2 thousand, 3 thousand...." It seemed like the surges were lasting about 60-90 seconds, which from what I read, I was already in the late stages, but we weren't sure. It was also tough to get an accurate count because I was never really sure when the surges were exactly over...but it didn't matter, we figured out the birth was happening for real.

David then called Di, and she advised that he make some tea for me and that we put on the relaxation CD. I lied on the bed, trying to get a little more shut-eye, but as the surges got more intense, I had to really focus and breathe in and out slowly. It never was "painful," just a tight sensation, but the pressure on my pelvis was slightly uncomfortable, and my back ached with each surge. Again, I just felt like I needed to poop constantly, guess the baby might already be engaged at that point.

As the surges came more frequently, I started pacing around the house. David reminded me to eat something, but I didn't really feel like it. He passed me a plate of Jacob's crackers, I munched on them and thought they tasted bland, so I ransacked the fridge for some cheese and ham and had a hearty little snack, amidst the surges! ;-)

Finally, at about 11:30 AM, I thought that the surges were getting so intense that it might be hard for me to walk around much. So, I told David that we needed to go to the hospital. He called my brother to come to pick us up, gathered up the suitcase, and helped me downstairs as I clutched on two pillows. I wanted to bring the pillows from home as I know they'd be much more comfortable than the ones at the hospital.

After a brief mix-up with my brother pulling into the wrong driveway, we were on our way. My mom asked if I was in great pain, and I told her not to use that word. My brother took the opportunity as a legitimate excuse to drive like an ambulance driver, which is the only way he drives. Still, we appreciated his good-hearted concern for us.

The hospital is just a 10 minutes' walk from our place, but it's hard to get to via car. We got there at about 12 PM and went upstairs to the labor ward. The ward sister said we had just missed Di, who had gone down a different lift. But we stayed cool.

The mid-wife introduced herself, she looked relatively young and was very friendly. She then put me on EFM, I couldn't wait to get off. I found that the most comfortable position was leaning against the side of the bed or sitting on the birthing ball. Being strapped on the bed for 20 minutes was certainly not what I had in mind. As each minute passed while I was on the bed, I felt the desire to get into water. Still, I wasn't feeling "pain," but there's certainly discomfort. I kept using the long breathing method through each surge, but my pelvis' pressure was getting quite annoying. I thought if I get into the birthing pool, the water should take some of the pressure off. David called Di to see when I could get into the birthing pool, and she said any time I wished. She was on her way back to the hospital.

I had initially thought I'd be so inhibited that I would feel awkward taking my clothes off and giving birth naked in the pool in front of hospital staff and the doctor. To my own surprise, I didn't care at all. I stripped away my clothes and got inside the pool as fast as I could. The warm water did make me feel better.

I had no concept of how much time had passed, and in the back of my mind, I was hoping that the labor should take 6 hours, that's how long an average HypnoBirthing labor usually takes. "So, if I really felt the surges only at about 7:30 AM, 6 hours from then would be about 1:30 PM…okay, maybe it'll take a little longer, so perhaps 8 hours, and that would be 3:30 PM…," I said to myself, and subconsciously, I had 1:30 PM or 3:30 PM as my "target time." I kept my eyes shut and floated on the water, I heard Di's voice, she got there. Both she and David held onto my arms and allow me to float around with my head staying above water.

I was still doing the long breathing, but now I could feel something really wanting to come out. Di asked me to go along with what my body told me, and I said, "My body is telling me to push." So, I started bearing down. I guess no one expected me to get to this stage so soon, the mid-wife hadn't even had a chance to do a vaginal examination. She had asked me if she could do it right after the EFM, but I really didn't feel like someone poking around down there, and I didn't want any disappointing news about a small dilation, so I never agreed to a VE.

It was really helpful to have Di next to us, she reminded me, again and again, to relax and take a cleansing breath between surges, and I was amazed at myself that I could keep my eyes closed, stay calm and block out whatever that was going on in the room.

The birth was imminent. I grunted and breathed down with each urge to push, but it didn't seem like I was going anywhere, I felt something was "stuck." Suddenly, Di asked, "Is that the baby?" And I said, "I think so!" Perhaps everyone saw something… I later learned that my membrane was visible, it never broke, and I pushed the baby out with the membrane intact. I think that's the reason why I felt like something was stuck. One end of the membrane was floating outside my vagina, but I couldn't get it and the baby out together without some extra help. It felt like forever.

Dr. Tseng arrived. I heard him said something about "pushing," and Di reminded him that I was simply "bearing down." ;-) All I remember hearing him say clearly was, "If you feel like you need to tear, it's okay." Strangely, that was very reassuring, as if I now had the permission to really push the baby out! I started pushing hard, and Di and David helped me through each surge by guiding my birthing song (grunts.) Dr. Tseng had to tear my membrane by hand, and within seconds, the baby's head was out. The next couple of seconds seemed a little out of control, I just felt like something slipped out all of a sudden. It was surreal. And here she is, little Ariah was right there!

She looked tiny, and she appeared "greyish," probably because she hadn't been "warmed up" yet. She had a small head, which was all eyes at this point, I couldn't believe how much she looked like me.

All I could mutter was "baby, baby," and I wanted to put her on my chest, but Dr. Tseng warned that the umbilical cord was short so I could only let her rest on my tummy. The cord was clamped and cut after it stopped pulsating,

David immediately tried to warm Ariah up by putting her on his bare chest. The nurses helped me out of the water, and I delivered the placenta on the bed within minutes.

Dr. Tseng announced that the time of birth for Ariah was 1:47 PM, everyone commented on how quick it was, especially for a first-time mom. I didn't realize that we had only been in the hospital for less than 2 hours at this point, but news spread quickly, and when my mom popped in to see us, she said everyone at the nurses' station was talking about how fast the birth was.

I had a small tear, Dr. Tseng stitched me up and gave me an injection to help my uterus contract. I felt pretty good and was ready to walk to the hospital room. Apparently, that was against hospital protocol, I had to be wheeled to the room instead. ;-) The nurse waiting at the room was amazed to see me arrive without any "attachment." She asked, "no epidural?" And the orderly who wheeled my bed there answered proudly for me, "No, she did waterbirth!"

To me, the entire labor and birthing process felt really more like a tedious physical activity, like an intense game of tennis or a long swim against the current, but not a really a medical process. I almost felt like I could go back to work the very next day. ;-) The same can't be said about motherhood, which I soon experienced. That is a completely out of control experience. :-O (Jen Tsai)

I had the privilege and thrill of attending all three of Jen and Dave's births. Actually, only two because the second baby was birthed so quickly that I never made it to the hospital on time. I loved that Jen stayed so focused on what her body wanted to do and that Dave protected her space. At the third birth, I remember that Jen was laboring in the tub and starting to bear down—breathe her baby out—and the nurse requested a vaginal exam to check the progress. Dave denied this request and told her to call the doctor, as the baby was coming quickly. The nurse replied that she could not call without doing an exam. He said, "Fine, you can receive the baby but no VEs."

When we were shifted to the postnatal ward after the birth, a nurse came rushing in, loudly congratulating Jen and Dave and explaining how the TV and air-con remotes worked and how to call for assistance. Dave calmly took the wee one into the bathroom for a quieter environment. Noises are so loud to babies after they emerge from the womb; they are used to water-muted sounds. After the nurse left, she came back to discuss the menu items loudly. Dave took the baby back into the bathroom. The nurse noticed and asked what was wrong. I explained that the baby would prefer quiet voices and primarily those of Mom and Dad. She understood, quieted her voice, and I hope she carried on in this way with other parents in the future.

Vaginal exams are very uncomfortable during labor. (Actually, come to think of it, they are always uncomfortable—in labor, pregnant, or not.) There are other ways to determine progress. One study by midwives found that 89 percent of women have a red line that appears on the sacrum. As it progresses up the crease on the woman's body, it's a clear indicator of how many centimeters her cervix has opened.

https://www.lamaze.org/Connecting-the-Dots/Post/the-red-purple-line-an-alternate-method-for-assessing-cervical-dilation-using-visual-cues

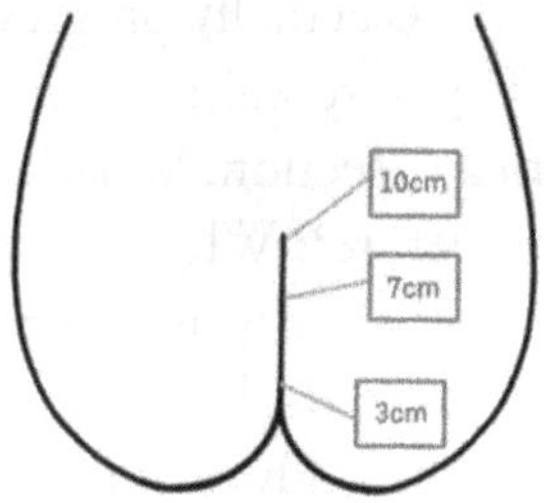

Artwork by Megan Tan

C-SECTIONS AND VBACS

Studies and guidelines are now being published that show the importance of waiting before inducing C-sections and reducing cesarean rates. The WHO states that only 12–15 percent of all labors require medical interventions. That's not cesareans—that's all interventions. The cesarean rate in the US is currently 32 percent.

Hi Di, my first pregnancy was C section and I'm aiming for VBAC for my 2nd. Most nurses & doctors were trying to scare me, saying there's a possibility of uterine rupture, and worry that the gap between 1st pregnancy & 2nd pregnancy was too close (less than 2yrs). When I was labouring, they kept asking if there was any pain at my previous C section wound. So frequently that I kind of imagined the pain came from the wound, instead of the contraction. And they persuaded to burst my water bag because of the fear of uterine rupture (again?), and building more fear in me when they started to schedule for C section when I was actually progressing! So unmotivating and they were waiting for me to say "I give up" and want a C section. What's wrong if you have a C section before?? What's wrong if the gap was close?? Why repeatedly asking about my previous C section? Yes, I do have a birth plan. But I would say they took advantage of me, and I'm glad to channel my frustration and make it as motivation and strength to go thru labour and

VBAC successfully. On a happier note, managed to skin-to-skin, delay cord-cutting, latch on immediately after birth. :)) Purposely hold on to baby long enough and refused to let go. (Nur Afifah Bt Mokhtiaruddin, Malaysia)

I had both babies by C section. A little disappointing, but from my 1st I believe it's due to my own lack of knowledge and the need to quickly get the IV plugin to stop the VE. I succumbed to a C section, but for my 2nd, although a C section, in the end, I was glad I experienced a trial of labour all according to my birth plan. Thanks to my supportive gynae for providing me the opportunity to attempt a VBAC. He knows I hate the plugs and VEs. Thus, he instructed the labour ward not to bother me without his permission. And even after 40hrs of labour with no progress of dilation (0cm) and liquor is low as water bag had burst at home, my gynae remained positive and let me decide to continue labouring or otherwise as the baby is fine and not in any distress. I had given in to C section only because of no progress despite all that me and my doula's attempts to naturally augment birth. So, I was a happier mummy giving birth at 40weeks plus 4. Oh, and I like it how he allowed food throughout and when I thought I may have uterine rupture he actually told me I will be fine and risk is low unlike the labour ward Drs. who kept scaring me with the rupture… (Angwyqween Rush Wosaini, Malaysia)

I had the pleasure of working with Dr. Park in Seoul, Korea, at her birthing center, Yeon and Nature. I trained her midwives in HypnoBirthing and the support of natural labor and birth. After the training, her cesarean rates dropped from 15 percent to 7 percent in one month.

It's all about educating the maternity care providers about natural birth. They all learned what to do for medical emergencies but have failed to learn what to do when birth goes as nature intended. Most have not observed a woman laboring from beginning to end. They only arrive at the end of the labor to receive the baby. Most of them feel the need to do something and assist the baby's emergence from the birth path, increasing the risk of tearing. Dr. Park found that if she let the baby rotate on its own, without her assisting in turning the baby manually, the perineum remained intact.

HANDLING AND PERMISSION

I complained before to my gynae regarding a labour ward doctor. He insisted I have a VE during one false alarm. I had already told her to be very gentle, but she was so rough I ended up with bad itch down there, and she was like a psycho handling me. I noted that to my gynae during a follow-up appointment, and he took it seriously enough that subsequent false alarms saw only specialists or midwives handling me. Because these labour ward Drs. are all somewhat inexperienced and don't understand what it means to be gentle. I just wish labour ward Drs. are trained to be more compassionate and are prepared to be gentle with our nether regions. Sad when it's a midwife who is so much better… And these Drs. depend too much on machine.

One midwife who handled me could even tell when I was having light or intense contractions by touching my tummy. And the midwife reminded me that VE is not absolutely necessary, but if I want to, just ask for a midwife because they are gentler…Caucasian lady, forgot her name. Very nice…

I wrote in feedback forms. And they did respond and call me back me, but were blaming each other's department, ha-ha. (Angwyqween Rush Wosaini, Singapore)

In my classes, I encouraged mothers to require the care providers to ask permission to touch their lady bits and to do so gently. This is a very sacrosanct area of our bodies, and we should be respected. It may not be taught in medical school; however, women can be their best advocates to demand respect.

INFLUENCES VERSUS INFORMATION

Congrats on having the opportunity to present Di, don't know whether I can be present or not but hope to, though. Would a birth attendant's voice be considered too? I'd like for doctors to not use the scans as a tool for induction, to unduly influence clients on the dangers which are not there, and to influence them to go for unnecessary scans, basically to stop lying to clients. To stop using excuses to induce, "low fluids" (unspecified low levels which in reality are not unduly low); "big baby" leading to shoulder dystocia (without any pelvimetry done before pregnancy and can flippantly give a 3.5kg weight as a cutoff point), pointing to a "lowered fetal heart rate" as a reason for induction (even though heart rate is averaging at 140), to stop routine episiotomy, to have skills to do breech birth and twin birth, and for those skills to be updated.

To advise clients on proper nutrition, dietary advice, and other suggestions to improve maternal outcomes instead of prescribing drugs and more tests and C sections.

To stop using induction routinely and to use inductions knowingly to push clients into undergoing a C sect.

To stop pretending to go along with clients' natural birth plan only to revert to the usual high intervention routine on labour day itself. (Fadillah Yusope, Singapore)

INFORMED AND POETIC BIRTH

I've known you forever
My ancient little one
Though you may have just arrived
I've known you since the dawn of time
The first time that I saw your face
I remembered you, I know this place
I can feel it deep within my core
I've been in love with you before
My baby, my beloved child
In me, you've lit a dormant fire
I'm so excited to start this round
Reunited with you on earthly ground
Here it starts, my little friend
The joy of life has just begun! (Ruth Li)

May 5, 2012

Our sweet and considerate Winifred sent out a few signals that she'd be coming soon, and her arrival went remarkably according to plan. She has been a wonderful baby who seems incredibly wise for her zero years and astoundingly aware of everything around her.

A few signs she sent to let us know that she was coming soon:

- Sat, April 14 (38 weeks) – first show with contractions (Mom, you might want to pack your hospital bag now)

- Sat, April 21 (39 weeks) – more show (Are you ready?)

- Sun, April 22 – lots more show and menstrual-like contractions starting (Seriously…)

- Mon, April 23 (39 weeks, 2 days) – (Here I come!)…

The contractions started around 7 AM on a Monday morning. I was pretty sure this was the real thing, even after all the false starts, as they were regularly coming (even as I tried to sleep through them), and were somehow different than all the practice ones before. Norm and I went ahead through the morning routine as if nothing were going on, with him and his cousins (who had just arrived to help with baby the day before) taking Jasper off to school while I stayed home. We didn't tell anyone we were pretty sure this was the day, just in case it wasn't.

I spent the morning taking care of household chores before attending my 39-week prenatal appointment, with contractions regularly coming throughout. I told Dr. Paul that I thought this was it, and he said it looks like things may be moving along. But of course, he had said the exact same thing at my previous appointment, so I left still not entirely convinced (or rather, convinced but irritated about not being validated). I felt a bit nauseated but went ahead and had a quick lunch at Cedele anyway, not wanting to labour on an empty stomach, then headed home.

That afternoon Norm took our guests and Jasper to the zoo as planned (my only condition was that he would not take everyone to the water park, lest I need them to hurry home and then have to wait while he gets everyone showered first). With everyone gone, I had the place to myself to labour in peace and quiet. I opened the windows and made myself a protein shake (on Di's suggestion). Then I did a rainbow relaxation session. It was a beautiful, breezy day.

Afterward, I moseyed around the house, taking care of whatever little details I could think of, then sat down on the birth ball and watched an episode or so of Frasier. It's just not as funny when you're in labour, so I turned it off and sang to our baby instead.

By about 3:00, the contractions seemed to be adopting the same cluster pattern as my previous labour. 2-3 contractions with 2-3 minutes between, and 6-8 min between clusters, and they were getting a bit more intense. By 4:00, I decided, with traffic and prep time, it was time to head to the hospital. The contractions were getting a little tougher to manage, and I felt like I could use a nice dip in the birthing pool. I called Di and Norm to say it's time to move. (Norm and company were, of course, at the zoo's water park).

Around 5:00, Norm and everyone else arrived home, and we got ready to go with a lot of luggage. Norm suggests I trim it down, and I refused, being a mother in the process of giving birth and all. We took Jasper and our relatives to hang out at the pool. Jasper was a bit upset about us leaving, but it worked out beautifully to give him the exciting, new Lightning McQueen Lego car we'd been saving for just that moment, and then he happily kissed us goodbye.

I told Di to meet us at the hospital. On the way out of the condo, Norm told me he's confident that I'm going to do great this time, which made me feel a little less nervous. I had a cluster of contractions lasting from the time we walked out to catch a cab to the time we arrived at Mt. Alvernia. Norm was officially timing this one (though I didn't note what the official timing was).

At 6:05, we checked into the hospital. Di had already arrived and was setting up the birth pool. Norm sets up the iPod and relaxation music, then goes to register and pay for the fee for bringing in a pool, our private maternity room, and the rest of the birth charges. I try to relax on the bed through and after the 20 minutes of fetal monitoring. It is a bit tough to ride through each cluster in the new hospital setting, with all the other "check-in" procedures going on, but I try to just let my body go with the flow, knowing the clusters' pattern and trying to expand with each one. Norm comes back just in time to find out that my cervix is dilated only 3, maybe 4, cm. I look at him, knowing he's thinking the same thing I am: shit, not again! (This was quite reminiscent of my previous birth, where each measurement revealed a much earlier stage than the intensity suggested to us.)

Norm rubs my back during the contractions, which helps me relax through them as we wait for the birth pool to be full. As soon as it is ready, I get in quick as I can. It feels like sinking into a gentle, warm hug, and suddenly the labouring I'm doing is comfortable and manageable again. Di turns the lights in the bathroom off, and there is only the light now from a few lamps in the delivery suite. It's a pleasant, peaceful environment.

Di goes down to Subway to get us something to eat while Norm changes into swim shorts. He takes what feels like an irritatingly long time to do so but finally joins me in the tub. Di comes back and feeds both of us bites of sandwich while we labour ("I don't think I've ever fed a couple dinner while they labour before"). I start needing to moan to get through them, and I sit across from Norm with my legs around his waist so I can spiral my hips. He runs his fingers up and down over my body in a soft touch massage, and in this way, we ride through these very intense surges. The surges have now, in fact, started feeling more like waves rushing over my body than contractions, and I have no real choice but to go with them to get through them. Di helps direct my voice lower, which seems to help also.

Di says to let her know if I feel like birth breathing, and I tell her I think I'm still quite far off from that. Having obviously attended a few more births than I, gives me an "okay... yeah, whatever you say..." look in response. Maybe 1-2 clusters later, I quite suddenly feel I need to be birth breathing instead. I tell Di, and she suggests I turn over onto my tummy. As I do so, something inside of me snaps, both literally and mentally. (The pop [and rush] I felt must have been my waters releasing, and I must have hit transition at that point because suddenly I felt like a crazed horse, ready to do anything necessary to get out of the experience.) All of a sudden, everything collapses—this whole calm HypnoBirthing charade I feel like I've been putting on is gone. Di gets down in front of me, calling me by name and saying something motivational, but I don't remember what. I tell her this hurts, and I'm done with this, and I'm ready for the epidural now. I can't do this. She says it's too late, I'm already there, I'm already doing it. I tell her I need to bite something.

I wish I had a wooden spoon. I bite my fingers instead, then Di gives me her shirt. I'm not sure it'll be as good as my own bony hands, but it ends up being a fine substitute ("I've never given a labouring mum my shirt to bite before"). Someone wants to do a VE, which is fine, so long as I don't have to move. Norm shifts me over a couple of inches so they can reach. It is confirmed, though I already know that I'm 10cm. Norm hugs me from behind, Di holds my hands in front, and I feel loved and supported but still in a lot of pain.

Like a horse whisperer calming a crazed mare, Di grounds me and helps me settle into a rhythm of birth breathing, and I can very clearly feel baby making her decent. The panic of transition is gone as quick as it came. With each rush, I press her further down with my breath and voice, trying to relax my body and let it do what it was designed to. Di helps again to direct my voice lower to help move baby down. Norm continues to run his fingers up and down my sides from behind. I can feel baby bulging down, and with 1-2 very intense clusters, I can reach down and feel her head already starting to emerge (Wow that didn't take long at all). Suddenly I feel a terrible stinging in front. My body makes the decision to quickly flip back over onto my back to prevent a tear. (It's only in retrospect that I realised what happened here and why I flipped, at the moment it was entirely instinctual) and her head fully emerges in one surge, no tears.

Oh, what a relief! And oh look, Dr. Paul is here ("Doctor, you've got to move your office here, they've got Subway, you know.")! Someone has a torchlight illuminating the pool, and Norm uses his hand to shield my eyes from the bright light. Di reminds me to keep my hips under the water now that the baby's head is out. I reach down and feel her head with my hands and wait for the next surge. In the next surge out slides her big, wrinkly body and Dr. Paul helps to pull her to my chest. ("There you are!") Here, at last, our big girl is here at last! She perks right up and picks her head up to find daddy and me and take a quick look around before she commences crying. Norm and I are amazed at what happened and how very different it was this time around. Here is our baby girl!

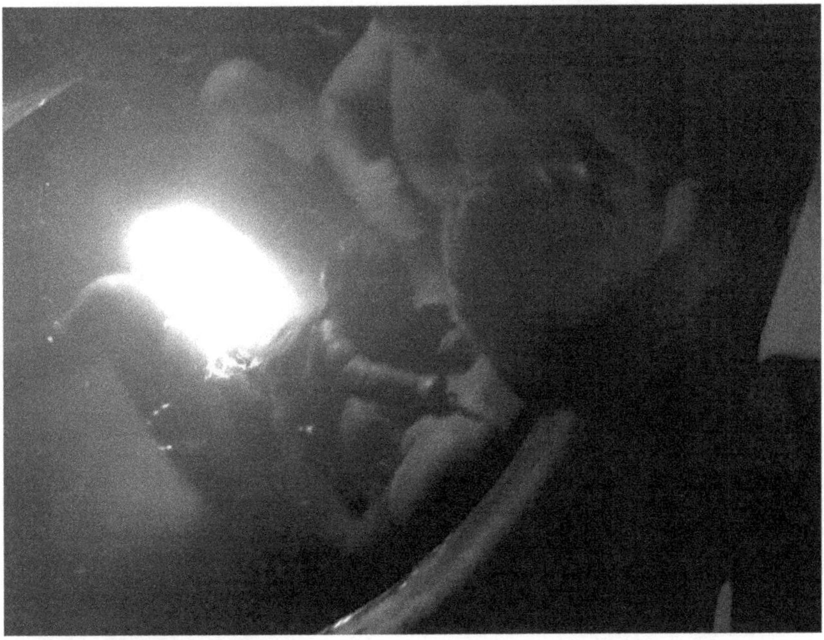

We rest in the tub for a while with our new little (big) baby. Norm is on the phone with our friends, XT and Ying, and asks them to come and pick up the rest of the family on the way. After a little while, we decide to make our way to the bed for the birth of the placenta. Dr. Paul confirms that the cord has stopped pulsing, and after an awkward attempt to get out of the tub with the short umbilical cord still attached, he goes ahead and cuts it for us.

Once snuggled comfortably on the delivery room bed, I ask Di how the breast crawl works. It's quite simple, and we just put our sweet little girl on my tummy. Within a few minutes, she wiggles her little self up to my breast and is latched on, snacking happily. The family and friends arrive, and Di goes to get Jasper and bring him in. He looks and confirms that it is indeed a mei mei (little sister) we have (actually no one had bothered to check until then), and is quite impressed by the umbilical cord.

Di is emptying the tub bucketful by bucketful, and Norm is horrified now that the lights are on and he can see how very red the water he was sitting in was (when the lights were still off he was flicking bits of vernix away from him, thinking that was as gross as it gets…). We let baby finish her first meal, and then the nurse weighs her—4.2 kg! (in Mickey Mongan's voice: My body makes—and births—big babies.)

Di heads off, and I put some clothes on to greet our friends and family waiting for us as we transfer to our postpartum room. Norm, Jian Qiang, Ai Xia, and Jasper stay until Jasper and our sweet new baby are both fast asleep in my lap—an exciting day for both of them! It feels like she has been a part of this family from the beginning.

15 days later, we finally name her Winifred (joy, blessed, peaceful) Zhen Ping (calm, peaceful, smooth, even).

Another glorious birth I had the pleasure to attend. Being able to observe Ruth's complete abandonment of the needs of her body and her baby and birth baby Winnie gently into our world is a memory I will always treasure.

I find it lovely to follow all the families I doula'd for on social media. They grow ever so fast. Ruth and Norm's babies are almost all grown up!

UNIQUE YET EQUAL

I would like medical caregivers (O&Gs*, doctors, midwives and nurses) to treat subsidized and non-subsidized equally and inform each patient what are they doing to us and give us a choice (too much to ask for? hehe)

*Obstetric And Gynaecological (Suhailah T Umm Sulaiman, Singapore)

Would love doctors and nurses to remember that the birth to each mom is unique and special, and it should not be just a job/process that they follow out of sheer habit. In their mind, it may be professional, but in the labouring mom's mind, she never wants to be just another patient. (San San Lee, Singapore)

I don't like doc to laugh at my every single suggestion… It makes me feel stupid! (Nurul Nutela, Malaysia)

I don't think we need a study to prove that this type of behavior is unacceptable.

Please tell me what you're doing and give me a chance to agree/disagree to it, please stop rushing me to birth my baby, please allow me to show you what an amazing thing a woman's body is! And how smart babies are during birth! (Danielle Sweetman, Malaysia)

Ah, what a blessing this would be! Great sentiment!

ANOTHER HYPNOBIRTHING LOVE STORY NADIA'S BIRTH STORY

It was 10.00 PM when my husband Fraser just got in the door after being on the Singapore flyer only an hour earlier. He was just in time because at 10.30 PM, I started getting very intense surges, which were 2 minutes long and 2 minutes apart. I was ready to have my first baby, and my bag wasn't even packed. Fraser learnt a lot about multitasking that night. He was running around trying to pack my bag, periodically massaging my back, as well as calling Dr. Paul Tseng and Lauren (my doula).

Meanwhile, I was rolling around on my birth ball and breathing deeply as I had learnt to do in the HypnoBirthing classes. It was clear to me, Lauren, and Dr. Paul that it was time to go to the hospital. I only made it as far as the lobby before I was on all fours again, roaring like a lion! When I made it to the car, my waters released, and by midnight we were at the hospital with Lauren arriving at the same time. I really thought there was a chance the baby could be born in the car!

Upon arrival at the hospital (Thomson Medical Centre), Dr. Paul told me that I was

fully dilated, and I was going to meet my baby very soon. I started out on all fours and then moved to a birthing stool to allow gravity to work its magic. Fraser was massaging my back, and Lauren was doing light touch massage on my arms while giving me gentle words of encouragement to breathe my baby down. As each surge got more and more intense, I got very vocal and primal, breathing deeply between each one. Everything moved so fast, and I got to the stage where I felt an overwhelming urge to push. The HypnoBirthing classes taught me to listen to my body and do what felt right for me, so I pushed hard for my baby to emerge. Fraser was told that she would come out with the next surge, so he made a hilarious attempt to put on latex gloves that were far too small. We all had a good giggle! He then received Anya and put her straight on my chest at 12.33 AM.

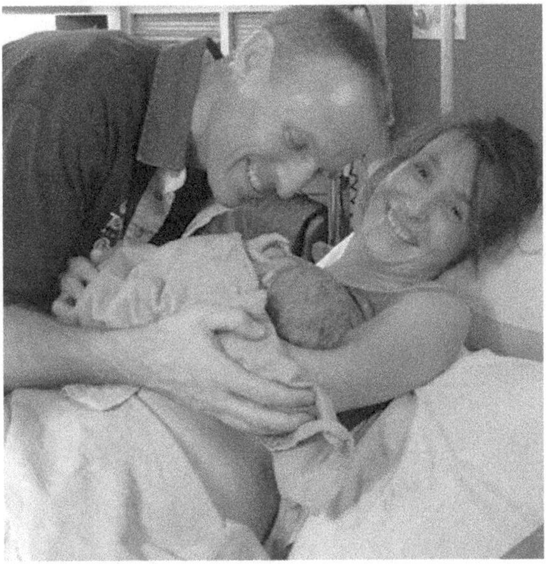

I squealed with delight at the sight of our bundle of joy. I couldn't wipe the grin across my face, and mummy and daddy fell in love immediately. My labour was unbelievably quick and an amazing experience that I will never forget. HypnoBirthing taught me to release all my fears surrounding childbirth and really believe in my ability to birth my baby in the most positive way. Fraser, Lauren, and Dr. Paul Tseng all helped me to have the natural birth that I envisioned, for which I am truly grateful. I feel that Anya got the best possible start in life.

HypnoBirthing is a great way to prepare for birth. The course also provides great coping tools that apply to your entire life.

IN MEMORY

Marie (Mickey) Mongan is not a book, a curriculum, an icon, or a legacy. She was a force that came from the universe with wisdom and knowledge that only God could have given. She was a vessel of divine enlightenment. Marie Mongan is and will continue to be an undeniable, irreplaceable warrior for women, childbirth, and our instinctive ability to give birth as we were created to do and intended from the very beginning of our creation. She was a courageous advocate, a light in the darkness. Marie Mongan wrote the New Testament of giving birth.

The Mongan Method was created by a woman for women through her own experiences, not only through observations and statistics. Marie Mongan envisioned it. Her goal was to dehypnotize our society of years of fear that no longer applies. She taught us not only to reframe prior birth experiences but also to erase the negative limbic imprints passed down from generation to generation. She did not teach meditation or instruct women to be in a meditative state. She said she did not teach how to have a baby; birthing couldn't be taught. Instead, she guided parents back to their instincts. Marie Mongan did not teach how to cope with labor, endure it, or the mechanics. She guided parents back within themselves to their own natural instincts. Mickey's insight and guidance helped parents change the negative programming of the past experiences of generations before us so that they could envision intrinsic labor and birth—to tap into their innate ability to labor and birth calmly and comfortably. The fear of labor today is unfounded because we no longer live in the same society as those past fears. The births of the generations before us are not the births of today. Childbed fever no longer exists. We no longer wear corsets, twilight sleep has been eliminated, and forceps or vacuum extractions abandoned.

Today, families choose where they give birth, how they give birth, and who attends when they give birth. Marie Mongan paved the way for a new perspective on labor and birth. She cemented a foundation that birth is instinctual, organic, and natural. She created a philosophy of life that has guided parents through labor and birth, as well as throughout life. Marie Mongan changed our minds! She did not create a technique or just a tool. It is a redirection back to whom we are designed to be—reconnecting the mind and body to work as one. Returning the labor process and the moment of birth to its sacred beginning is deeply rooted within us.

Marie Mongan has accomplished what we all say we want ourselves; she left this world a better place than how she found it. She left us with a better birthing environment, a better understanding of our bodies and our abilities. She taught us to ask the simple question, "Why?" and how to respond gracefully. She showed us how to stand in our truth and draw from the power within us. She encouraged us, challenged us, inspired us, and loved us. She taught us to take responsibility as women for our bodies and our care. We are not girls, she would say. You are women, and you must act like a woman to be treated as a woman; if you call yourself a girl, you will act like a girl and be treated like a girl. Marie Mongan was a trailblazer, warrior, and pioneer. She embodied strength and knowledge that is indescribable. Her wisdom was never-ending. She saw it all more clearly, even without physical sight. It all just made sense to her, and it was her goal to help us see it.

Many have copied and plagiarized her work. Some say they will carry on her vision, but they do not see her vision because they are blinded by their greed, ego, and self-serving, self-absorbed intentions. Marie Mongan's work will continue to live not by them but by the people's lives she changed, the babies born into this world with her guidance. Her work will continue from the seeds she planted within us and watered them until they grew deep roots. Her work will continue because it is a universal force that flows effortlessly through us as we breathe. My only hope and intention are to live a life that is worthy of her respect and blessing. To continue to be loyal to her, carry on as she had told me to do, and not move on without her but pick her up in my arms and carry her with me. She friended me, mothered me, mentored me, trusted me, and believed in me. I am thankful, humbled, and honored to have been in the same room. When in her presence, you felt as if you were standing on holy ground, you knew each time that you were experiencing something life-altering, and your future was about to change. May we all strive to be just an ounce of who she was; and if we do, we, too, will leave this world a better place.

So who was Marie "Mickey" Mongan? She was kind, loving, compassionate, passionate, empathetic, sympathetic, creative, wise, intelligent, strong, courageous, driven, motivated, and encouraging. She was a fearless warrior, trailblazer, fighter, and advocate, who was full of forgiveness and grace. Her passing is not only a loss to the birthing world but to humanity itself. Our world will forever be altered, completely shifted on its axis. May we all strive to live up to the example she has set—to be the best we can be.

Rest in peace, Mickey. You will never be forgotten.

SLOW STEPS TO BIRTH CHANGES

My 4th baby birthing experience is quite good despite the EFM machine. I nearly gave up in the finale and asked the doc to vacuum my baby as I can't push anymore. But the doc calmly said to me, "Don't worry, no need to push. The baby will find his way out." and soon after that, baby makes his way out. The doc saved me from epidural and stitches. (Siti Sohailah, Malaysia)

Yeah! A patient doctor!

During my 6th birth, I was allowed to sit (and wasn't strapped to CTG), hugging my husband, who rubbed my back non-stop for 3 hours till shortly before my baby was born. Think the doc/nurses were so easy on me because I had all 5 babies with them previously. Made their work easier, too, I guess. I imagine it would be better if I can do that in water. We will see in Oct, currently 24 weeks pregnant with no 7. (Ros Fatihah Muhammad, Malaysia)

I don't know about her previous five births but so thrilled she was "allowed" to labor freely, as she and her partner chose. I wish her all the best for a water birth option!

SECTION 5

Sexual Abuse and Childbirth

Since I have experienced sexual abuse and discovered how it affected my birthings, I feel it essential to provide information on how to support those who have experienced similarly. After I had been doula'ing for a while, I began to routinely and privately ask if the women had ever experienced sexual abuse. I found it easier to support them, as it always caused distress in one way or another during their labor. As the labor unfolded, many times, I could tell which mothers had been abused, even if they did not remember it or choose to share.

According to *On Trial: America's Courts and Their Treatment of Sexually Abused Children* (Beacon Press, 1989; 2d ed., 1991), Dziech and Schudson write, "The latest statistics indicate that 1 American female in every 3 or 4 is likely to be sexually victimized before she is 18 years old." One in five women have been sexually abused as children. I include studies and papers on how to support women who have been sexually abused.

https://www.wcsap.org/advocacy/focus-areas/pregnant-parenting-survivors

W24 survey shows one in five women have been sexually abused as children. https://mypr.co.za/w24-survey-shows-1-in-5-women-have-been-sexually-abused-as-the-metoo-trend-sweeps-social-media/

Providing Care for Survivors of Sexual Abuse during Childbirth
August 24, 2017 (Poslaneic 2017)

"Humiliating and Traumatic," these are the words from a survivor of sexual abuse when asked to describe her labour and delivery. All too often, women who have been sexually abused carry their wounds into the delivery room. And, all too often, these unresolved traumas rear their ugly heads and cause complications, from labour dystocia, to full blown anxiety attacks that result in a woman completely shutting down. These are some of the more challenging labours to manage.

According to the US Department of Health, one in four girls and one in five boys will be sexually abused before they turn 18. One in five women and one in 71 men will be raped at some point in their lives. This is in many ways a silent epidemic. Sometimes victims don't disclose their abuse to their care providers. The reasons vary, and can range from ongoing suffering of the traumatic effects of the abuse and avoiding reliving it, to a continuing sense of shame that victims may have never come to grips with.

What are some possible signs of sexual abuse?

According to *When Survivors Give Birth: Understanding and Healing the Effects of Early Sexual Abuse on Childbearing Women*, having a constellation of these symptoms can indicate a history of abuse. Having one or more of the following should trigger a red flag and considerations for a woman's care during childbirth:

Not able to feel fetal movement. Some women have "numbed" that part of the body.

Hyperemesis gravidarum
Chronic pelvic pain
Missed prenatal appointments
Panic with vaginal exams
Extreme anxiety with IV starts
Disassociation that manifests as if she's going into a trance

Many of these symptoms can understandably occur in women who don't have a history of sexual abuse, but when a woman has two or more, it's reasonable to suspect that such a history is possible. These symptoms can stem from PTSD, which is triggered by a woman's perception of loss-of-control, as well as the physical sensations that occur during pelvic exams, labour, and birth. By rushing through procedures, and not allowing the woman time to process (if possible), understand, and consent to what is happening to her body, we can inadvertently trigger a posttraumatic reaction.

Admittedly, the discussion of sexual abuse is a tough topic for those on either end of the conversation. We often just touch on the subject while reviewing women's admission histories, and then move on. Fortunately, we don't need the admission of abuse to employ strategies developed for survivors. It's actually much more common for caregivers to pick up on non-verbal cues and then tailor their care. A real tragedy is the guilt and shame survivors can feel after giving birth. So, like we would do for any woman, it's best to acknowledge the struggle of labour and birth, the strength a woman demonstrated, and the effort and precious reward she achieved.

What are interventions that nurses and other caregivers can provide?

Explain as much as you can in advance, for example, "If we run into an emergent situation there might be unfamiliar nurses coming in to help. I know this can cause anxiety, but I want to prepare you ahead of time in case it happens."

Always start with asking permission. From starting an IV to turning on the overhead lights, make sure to obtain permission before doing any procedures or making changes to the environment.

Go slowly with everything you do — this can be helpful in relation to a woman's fear of losing control. Fast movements can be triggers. This is especially important when uncovering a woman or assisting her with positioning.

Limit vaginal exams. These are especially traumatic and should be minimized. If a woman is having difficulty in relaxing enough to complete an exam, try making an agreement about when and why you can perform one. If a woman understands that the exams are being performed only when necessary, and with her consent, her anxiety is often more controllable during exams.

Minimize people in her room. She might have issues with nursing students or residents, especially if they are male. Obtain her permission before any new staff come into the room, unless there's an emergent situation.

What are things not to say?

Intrusive interest-prying for details or descriptions of the abuse

Minimizing the abuse: "Well, that's over now."

Exaggerated concern

Shock or disgust

Pity

What are good things to say?

"I can imagine that was very hard to share that with me. It takes a lot of courage to talk about and I respect you for doing that."

"Sometimes talking about these episodes can trigger strong feelings. How are you feeling right now?"

And, it's always essential to assess the woman's current well-being. "Do you feel unsafe in any aspect of your life?"

Not all survivors of sexual abuse have difficulty with pregnancy or childbirth, for some it can be empowering. For those who do struggle, recognize that we have a powerful opportunity to help them. We can communicate therapeutically to help change the woman's focus from feeling out-of-control. We can employ care practices to avoid the woman feeling re-traumatized. And we can set the stage to promote healing and bonding with the newborn. In many instances it's our tacit recognition and respectful and supportive care that facilitates healing, more than any words we could utter or medicines we could administer.

Where can I learn more?

When Survivors Give Birth: Understanding and Healing the Effects of Early Sexual Abuse on Childbearing Women–Simkin, Penny and Phyllis H. Klaus Seattle: Classic Day, 2011. Print.

National Sexual Abuse Hotline 1 800 656 HOPE

RAINN: Rape, Abuse, Incest National Network www.rainn.org.

SECTION 6

Planning a Pregnancy

When considering inviting a wee one into your life, you can take many essential steps to create an easier and more positive outcome.

EXERCISE AND PELVIC FLOOR

First, review your exercise regimen. Every person has different exercise requirements. Some need to exercise daily, others two or three times a week. I encourage you to find an activity that you enjoy. Look at all your options and what fits into your lifestyle. Consider joining a gym and discussing your needs with a trainer. Consider a TV or YouTube exercise show if you can stick to it. Another alternative is to join a hiking club or a softball team—anything that gets you out there, continuously motivated.

What can your partner do to help? Please discuss with your partner what your thoughts are and ask for their support either by joining in with you, finding a regimen you both can enjoy or, at the very least, being supportive emotionally and physically. Perhaps they can pick up some of the chores that are usually your responsibility to free up some of your time.

Good posture is essential throughout pregnancy. Get into the habit now of standing and sitting correctly. Align your shoulders over your hips and your hips over your ankles. Shoulders are not to be rolled back. This posture places your ribcage in front of your hips rather than over them.

It's always a great time to start pelvic floor exercises. You can use a trigger to remind you to do this daily, such as brushing your teeth. You want to be able to tighten and relax the pelvic floor muscles. Imagine holding back urine or not passing wind. These are the muscles you want to tighten and relax. When it comes time to birth, you want the pelvic floor relaxed, as it is an easier descent for the baby, plus it reduces your risk of tearing the perineum.

Studies show that men should also practice pelvic floor exercises. As a result, they have less risk of needing Viagra or having prostate problems.

Putting it down in writing, having a plan can help you get into a routine. To stay on track, keep it on your calendar, either daily or three times a week.

Activity 1

Create a plan for establishing regular and consistent exercise in your life.

Create a trigger for establishing regular pelvic floor exercises.

NUTRITION

Second, review your nutrition.

Starting with a healthy BMI helps promote fertility, healthy pregnancy, and baby.

To find your body mass index (BMI), multiply your weight in pounds by 705, divide the result by your height in inches, and divide again by your height. The result is your BMI. Get out your calculator.

For example, a woman weighs 150 pounds and her height is five feet six inches (sixty-six inches):

150 pounds × 705 = 105,750

105,750/66 = 1,602

1602/66 = 24 BMI

BMI	Weight Status
Below 18.5	Underweight
18.5–24.9	Normal
25.0–29.9	Overweight
30.0 and above	Obese

The body will have some fat stores during pregnancy. There is a purpose to these fat stores—to aid women during labor, as women usually do not eat much, and in the first early days when the baby is feeding every one and a half to two hours. Most women whilst breast-feeding are starving and have trouble keeping their thirst quenched.

BMI	Preferred Weight Gain
Below 19.8	28–40 lbs 13–18 kg
19.8 to 26	25–35 lbs 12–16 kg
26.1 to 29	15–25 lbs 7–11 kg
29.1 and above	15 lbs 11 kg

Diet Suggestions

What you eat three months prior to conceiving will affect your pregnancy and your baby.

According to a Harvard study, saturated fats from meat and dairy increase your risk of morning sickness.

Most women enter pregnancy with low iron stores. Therefore, 18 mg of iron each day is recommended. Some foods can help your body absorb iron from iron-rich foods; others can hinder it. To absorb the most iron from the foods you eat, avoid drinking coffee or tea or consuming calcium-rich foods or drinks with meals containing iron-rich foods. Calcium itself can interfere. To improve your absorption of iron, eat it along with a good source of vitamin C. Good sources are orange juice, broccoli, or strawberries, or eat nonheme iron foods with food from the meat, fish, and poultry group.

Info. Prenatal Diagnosis: My Fertility Guide. https://www.myfertilityguide.biz/prenatal-diagnosis/info-pws.html

Top Iron-Rich Foods List: Globalinfo247. https://globalinfo247.com/top-iron-rich-foods-list/

Excellent sources of iron-rich foods:

Beans and lentils
Tofu
Baked potatoes
Cashews

Dark-green leafy vegetables (spinach)
Whole grain and enriched bread
Shellfish
Organ meats
Pumpkin seeds
Quinoa
https://www.webmd.com/diet/iron-rich-foods#2

Folic acid prevents neural tube defects in the early stages of pregnancy. 400 mg of folic acid daily and great sources (not fortified)[123]:

Edamame
Okra
Spinach
Artichoke
Turnip greens
Broccoli
Asparagus
Brussel sprouts
Romaine lettuce
Escarole
Beets
Potato with skin
Avocado
Papaya
Orange juice
Beans
Lentils
Peas
Sunflower seeds
Peanuts
Liver

---

1 Dieticians of Canada. *Food Sources of Folate* (February 25, 2014).

2 Harvard School of Public Health Nutrition Source. *Keep the Multi, Skip the Heavily Fortified Foods* (n.d.).

3 The Spina Bifida and Hydrocephalus Association of Ontario. *Food Sources* (n.d.).

CHANGES TO INCREASE FERTILITY

Consider switching to boxers to increase sperm count. Eliminate caffeine, alcohol, medical and recreational drugs, processed meats, unnecessary fats, white foods, and sweets.

FERTILITY FOODS

Some foods are thought to increase your fertility. Please note that there are no studies to support these; however, I wanted to include them for your review.

Zinc

Magnesium

Vitamin E

Vitamin C and D for strong bones

Yams, which are rich in folate, as well as vitamins C and B_6

These vegetables contain diosgenin, a substance similar to progesterone, which can help stimulate ovaries to release one or more eggs each month.

Nuts and seeds—including almonds, walnuts, and pumpkin seeds—are excellent sources of fatty acids. Omega-3 and omega fatty acids are hormone regulators vital to a woman's fertility since a hormonal imbalance can interfere with ovulation.

Cruciferous vegetables—such as broccoli, cabbage, and cauliflower—contain vitamin A and a substance called diindolylmethane, which regulates the metabolism of estrogen, which is essential for keeping fertility hormones in check.

Oysters have the highest zinc content of any food. Zinc helps maintain a healthy menstrual cycle. However, zinc deficiency has been linked to decreased fertility since it can slow the production of good-quality eggs essential for conception.

Best foods to improve fertility. Fertility foods to eat: https://www.mothersspace.in/getting-pregnant/boost-your-fertility/fertility-foods/.

Berries, such as blueberries and raspberries, are exceptionally high in antioxidants, preventing cell damage and aging and helping to protect eggs and sperm. Protecting egg cells from the aging process is vital for enhancing conception for women who delay having a child.

Tea: Green tea and orange pekoe tea are both excellent fertility enhancers. Tea contains a high level of antioxidants that aid in healthy immune systems. Research has shown that women who regularly drink tea increase their chance of conception.

Foods rich in vitamin C: Fruits, especially citrus, help enhance fertility, especially in men. In addition, vitamin C plays a role in boosting the immune system and thus helps aid in a healthy conception.

Foods high in calcium: Calcium contributes to strong bones and is especially important for pregnant women to consume.

Vitamin B_6 and folic acid: Green leafy vegetables, nuts, and whole grains contain high levels of these nutrients. Vitamin B_6 is a reproductive hormone regulator, and folic acid helps prevent certain neural tube defects in the fetus.

Water is probably the most important thing to consume. The current recommendation is to halve your weight for the correct number of ounces per day. Example: If you weigh 120, drink 60 ounces of water per day.

Activity 2
Daily Diet Exercise

The following chart is calibrated for an average woman with average dietary needs. Please seek the advice of a naturopath or nutrition specialist to fine-tune your nutritional needs. Complete this throughout one week to ascertain where you need to adjust to maximize your fertility.

Daily Nutrition Log

Nutrient	Serving Equivalents	Required Servings	Your Servings	+ or –	Action Plan
Water	8 oz (220 ml) pure water	eight to twelve			
Veggies	1 cup (225 g) raw leafy vegetable ½ cup (110 g) raw or ½ (110 g) cup cooked non-leafy vegetable or vegetable juice	five to seven			
Nuts, seeds, and good oils	¼ cup (50 g) nuts or seeds 3 tbsp (45 ml) healthy oils: olive, nut, canola, and flax (not for cooking). Avoid safflower, sunflower, soy, and corn oil, as they are high in omega-6.	four			
Whole grains	½ cup (110 g) whole grains (cooked): rice, oats, wheat, barley, quinoa, spelt, etc. 1 slice whole wheat, rye, or other whole grain bread ½ cup (110 g) whole grain pasta cooked	three to five			
Fruits	1 medium-sized piece fresh fruit ½ cup (110 g) cut fruit ¼ cup (50 g) dried fruit 4 oz (110 ml) of 100 percent juice	three to four			
Legumes (beans)	½ cup (110 g) legumes (cooked)	two to three			
Protein (high quality)	4 oz (110 g) poultry 4 oz (110 g) fish (limit to three to six per week) 4 oz (110 g) red meat (limit to two per month) 1 medium-sized egg 8 oz (225 g) tofu	two to three			
Dairy (reduced fat)	1 cup (220 ml) milk, fortified soy milk, yogurt, and cottage cheese 1 oz (30 g) cheese	one to two			

Folic acid: Folic acid reduces the risk of neural tube defects and other congenital disabilities. The RDI for women 19 to 50 years old is 400 ug per day of folic acid in addition to folate provided through food. Supplementation, as part of a prenatal multivitamin, should begin one month before conception.

B12: Strict vegetarians and vegans should also take supplemental B12 to reduce the risk of neural tube defects. The RDI for women 19 to 50 years old is 2.4 ug per day.

Iron: Preconception iron status is important for reducing the risk of iron deficiency and anemia during pregnancy. The RDI for women 19 to 50 years is 18 mg per day.

ESSENTIAL OILS

There are essential oils considered helpful for fertility. Please seek the advice of a professional for application and dosages.

Clary sage
Geranium
Cypress
Thyme
Fennel
Roman chamomile
Ylang-ylang

DENTAL CARE

Another vital aspect to keep in mind is your dental care. Have your teeth cleaned every six months, floss daily, and brush at least twice daily. Gum infections are not merely in the mouth, as the bloodstream carries the infection to the rest of your body.

REVIEWING YOUR OWN BIRTH EXPERIENCE

How were you born? If your parents have not already shared their experience of your birth, ask them to share what happened. If there was any trauma or drama, consider regression therapy to clear the experience, enabling you to create another, more positive experience for you and your baby. www.birthpsychology.com

Activity 3

Your mother's story of your birth:

____

Your father's story of your birth:

____

What sense can you make of these stories?

____

What do you like about their stories?

____

What do you wish would have been different?

____

Do their stories relate to any of your current emotional reactions to events or conversations?

____

WELCOMING A BABY INTO YOUR LIFE

Some cultures intentionally seek out the baby spirit as they are planning a pregnancy. First, the mother meditates to find the name of the child that will be born into their family. Then the child is welcomed, even before conception, into their community.

Intention is a powerful tool to focus your mind on your goals. This exercise allows parents to envision and realize what they might want and expect in a child.

Activity 4

Take a few moments and make a list of all the attributes, virtues, and interests you want in the child you are creating to be in your life.

Now take a moment and reflect on the fact that you might not have the child you are envisioning. Be ready for whatever comes your way. Children have a mind of their own right from the start.

Activity 5

Write a list of all you have to offer the child you are welcoming into your family. Then create a definitive compilation that any child will want in their parent.

PRENATAL PARENTING

There are ten principles of prenatal parenting. More explanation can be found in the book *Prenatal Parenting* by Dr. Fred Wirth. Delve into these topics and learn how you can create a healthy, happy baby. While you are pregnant, the first easy step is to spend fifteen minutes several times a day with a fetal love break. A fetal love break is taking a few moments to focus on your baby within. Have an internal conversation with your baby, expressing your gratitude and joy anticipated in the life you will have together. Awareness of these principles honors the sacredness of the family and the intelligence of your unborn baby and helps you think of ways to become more peaceful during your pregnancy. For more information, visit the prenatal parenting website.

http://www.prenatalparenting.com/

The Ten Principles

- Your unborn child has more nerve cells and connections within its brain than an adult.
- Your baby shares your emotional experiences.
- You are the architect of your child's brain!
- As your baby's mother, you cannot hide your most intimate thoughts and feelings from your growing baby.
- Your baby has memories of his experiences before birth.
- Your baby communicates with you biochemically as well as through his senses.
- Your baby can feel, hear, smell, taste, and see before birth.
- Your baby develops consciousness and a sense of self separate from you before birth.

- Your baby's in utero experience sculpts the architecture of her brain, determining her behavior after birth and probably for the rest of her life.
- Each infant is born with a distinct temperament that may require specific parenting techniques for proper nurturing after birth.
- Your baby is born looking for meaningful relationships and knows how to develop them.

APPPAH. The Association of Prenatal and Perinatal Psychology and Health is the leading research and education source for understanding the awareness of the baby in the womb and at birth.

In the *Journal of Prenatal and Perinatal Psychology and Health* 31(3), spring 2017, Michael Appleton wrote:

> Dissonance disrupts bonding and attachment, disrupting what is often referred to by clinicians as the First Year Attachment Cycle. This cycle begins when a baby feels a need. As babies cannot satisfy their needs on their own, they become sympathetically aroused. If the need is gratified, the baby feels relief and relaxes. The repetition of this experience creates a foundation of trust in the relationship and the world as being places where needs get met.

An example of this would be the baby's hunger, cries, and is fed. Satiety brings relaxation. The baby becomes increasingly distressed and overwhelmed if the need is not met. If it goes on long or often enough, the baby collapses into resignation, and trust in a relationship / the world is lost. Neither relationship nor the world is experienced as safe. As we saw earlier, empathic mirroring of babies' stories is also a need, and insofar as this need is met, the attachment cycle is positively reinforced. Insofar as it is not met, the cycle is negatively reinforced. In the latter case, the baby's emotional expressions seem incoherent to the parents, that is, "I have tried feeding, rocking, distracting, nothing seems to work," and the parents' responses are incoherent to the baby. This throws the baby into an incomprehensible world where nothing feels safe or trustworthy.

Planning with mindfulness and awareness of the pregnancy and birth of your child makes a difference in who your child will be.

PARENTING STYLES

We are from different families, joining to create a new one. Each family has its parenting style, and now you need to discuss a combination or a new way of parenting that will suit the two of you together—compromising and combining until you get it right. I encourage you to read *The Science of Parenting* by Margot Sunderland. It will help you understand how your baby's brain develops and how best to promote strong and healthy individuals.

Activity 6

Here are a few philosophies to discuss and come to an agreement on.

- Choices in your maternity care provider.
- Active management versus expectant management style (discussed in further detail in the birthing section of this book).
- Birthing options.
- From planned cesareans to home water births.
- Conscious parenting or Gina Ford's philosophy—agree right from the start.
- Co-sleeping with your baby or sleeping in separate bedrooms?
- Breastfeeding? Read the benefits in the next section of this book.

AFFIRMATIONS FOR FERTILITY

Affirmations help develop the mind-body connection. The body follows the directions of the mind. Think about blushing in embarrassment; there is no physiological reason for the blood to rush to the face. It is a physical reaction to the emotion. When speaking to a crowd, some people get butterflies in the stomach—a physical response. The sympathetic (emergency room) and parasympathetic (healing room) systems are engaged in these scenarios. Negative emotions, like fear, create the flight-or-fight response in our body. Fear has value in the right situation; however, it stresses our bodies. Studies show that those who live in a constant state of stress are more likely to get sick. It affects us down to the cellular level in our immune system. Staying in more positive emotions helps us to create better health for ourselves. Like Pavlov's dogs, the more we practice, the easier it becomes to keep in positive emotions by utilizing affirmations.

There are six Ps that rule affirmations:

- plausible
- practiced
- personal
- positive
- present tense
- precise

Affirmations are better if kept short. They must be believable. Repeat them out loud in lots of three, three times a day. They must be about you. They must be what you do want, not what you don't want. For example, I don't want my baby to be born on Christmas Day. Most likely, this baby will be born on Christmas Day, as Christmas Day is the focus. Affirmations cannot be past or future tense. Make them as precise as possible. Cute story: I had a friend who wanted to invite a man into her life. She was looking for her life partner. She wrote down every attribute, virtue, and morals she wanted in this man. One of her list items was that she wanted him to be rich. She ended up marrying a man named Rich. She could have said she wanted a wealthy man, but wealth can be measured in many ways. She could have said she wanted a man with lots of money in the bank, but he would also have to be generous. The moral of the story? Be very precise.

Examples of affirmations for fertility:

My body is perfectly designed for conception.

Everything I need to conceive is already inside me.

My sperm will swim strongly to its goal.

My child will thrive physically and emotionally.

This IVF procedure will implant as it is meant to.

I encourage you to write your personalized affirmations to suit your desires, needs, and goals. It is a great exercise to get your mind to stay in the healing room.

Activity 7

Write affirmations regarding fertility, pregnancy, labor, birth, and parenting. Review, edit, and update them daily.

Activity 8

https://www.youtube.com/watch?v=-3mtFRjEVWc

View this documentary entitled *What Babies Want.* Reflect on the film and respond to these questions:

How do you feel about the story of the twins?

How can you reorganize your lives to welcome this baby into your lives?

What can you do to create a positive environment during pregnancy?

After watching this, does it change or reinforce your vision of your upcoming birth experience?

How much longer does it take for babies to integrate new information?

How do you feel about hospital births now? Does it seem to be the safest option?

What was your birth experience like? Is there any work you need to do to remove negative imprints?

Over the years, I have provided hypnotherapy to many couples experiencing fertility challenges. I have always encouraged these couples to consider these books to empower their pathway to parenthood. As a result, 80 percent of them achieved pregnancy within one year.

It's Conceivable by Lynsi Eastburn

https://www.amazon.com/Its-Conceivable-Hypnosis-Fertility-2nd/dp/1723485802/ref=sr_1_2?ie=UTF8&qid=1547854261&sr=8-2&keywords=lynsi+eastburn

The Three Keys to Conception by Lynsi Eastburn

https://www.amazon.com/Keys-Conception-Pregnancy-Against-Odds/dp/1544942273/ref=sr_1_1?s=books&ie=UTF8&qid=1549400927&sr=1-1&keywords=the+3+keys+to+conception

The Fertile Female by Julia Indichova

https://www.amazon.com/The-Fertile-Female-How-the-Power-of-Longing-for-a-Child-can-Save-Your-Life-and-Change-the-World/dp/B00J2LGVGU/ref=cm_cr_getr_d_rvw_txt?ie=UTF8

SECTION 7

Planning a Birth

Since birth experiences have such a significant impact on mothers and babies, on the next several pages, I'm sharing what I have learned through courses, reading, and experiences to aid those in looking for the best birth experiences possible. I encourage you to find a HypnoBirthing class near you. This course is designed to assist you to trust your body and understand that your baby can and will birth gently and easily.

In Singapore, eight hospitals provided maternity wards. Each had their own set of rules and ways of doing things. Most would allow doulas to attend the births, some would not. Some provided water births, others did not. Some required women to lay supine to birth, others provided birthing stools and foam floor mats. Birthing centers were not an option, and only one doctor would attend home births, Dr. Lai Fon Min. Midwives were required to be attached to a hospital to receive a license.

My point here is each doctor and hospital had their own set way of doing things. I believe this points to the fact that not all are practicing evidenced-based care; they are practicing to their individual preferences.

Women are consumers for birthing options. Women can make their choices known and create change in the maternity care they receive. Understanding all their options and why they would want to choose them is the key to having a joyful birthing experience.

As you read this section, I have included links to videos of beautiful births to invite you to envision such a birth. It's your birthright; go ahead, claim it, and make it your own experience. The more you view these births, the easier it becomes for you to believe that you can have this gorgeous birth experience. Give yourself permission, for you and your baby, to have a beautiful birthing experience.

Most of the videos are of water births. This is not because water births are the be-all and end-all of great birth experiences. It is because these births tend to be calmer and relaxed and are most likely to be uploaded to share. I tried to select videos that are short—five minutes or less.

In teaching my classes, I always started with an exercise to assist me in discovering parents' beliefs and help them assess where they are at the beginning of the class and compare at the end of the course what they continue to believe and what has changed.

Our beliefs are formed by our experiences in life and by those who have influence over us. Our long-term memory tracks all that has happened to us right from the beginning and stores it in our subconscious mind. Our own birth experience had an effect on our beliefs about birth. Ask your mother how you were born. This was your first lesson on what birth is all about. We are influenced by what we hear others say about birth, what we read, and what we see on TV and movies (and that's Hollywood and not birth as I know it).

Activity 1

Take a moment to answer these questions before flipping to the next page. Consider writing one adjective that best describes your beliefs about:

Pregnancy
Labor
Birth (the baby emerging from mother's body)
Parenting

Are your responses about pregnancy joyful, creative, and beautiful?

Are your responses about labor natural and your body working in perfect harmony with your baby?

And birth? A joyful welcoming for your baby?

Did you think about the baby at all in your responses?

Pregnancy, labor, and birth are not just about the mother.

Babies have all five senses at birth. They can see by twenty-four weeks and hear by twenty weeks; their central nervous system develops in the first trimester. They are tasting the amniotic fluid laced with intense flavors of the mother's diet. They are aware during their birth experience, creating a memory that will last a lifetime. Not a conscious memory, like what I had for breakfast this morning, but a sensory one, creating fore- and hindbrain connections shaping the way the baby's brain will develop. If you viewed *What Babies Want,* as suggested in the section about planning a pregnancy, the importance of planning the birth is crystal clear.

Babies are born with many connections to be made between the hind- and forebrain. If the baby is born violently, maltreated, or taken away from its mother, more hindbrain connections are made. The brain tries to wire survival conditions. If the baby is birthed gently and has direct skin-to-skin contact with the mother and father/partner, more forebrain connections are made, providing more creative learning opportunities.

Keep this list that you have created. After reading this and the next section of the book, take a look at your list. Have your beliefs been reinforced, or have they changed?

FINDING YOUR CARE PROVIDER

How best to find the care provider that is the right choice for you? Find out what your beliefs are first. Discover all your options for birthing, and decide which ones make the most sense for you.

Activity 2

Finding the correct maternity care provider for you will require research and soul-searching. The choice of your best friend might not match your needs. Here are some thought-provoking philosophies to guide you on your way. Answer these questions with either yourself, your doctor, or your partner. You can have multiple-choice responses.

Who is in charge of how your birth experience unfolds?
What position you labor and birth in?
What you wear during labor?
Who is with you in the labor room?
What pain relief options you use?
Medical interventions to speed labor up?
Choice of music?
When is the proper time to go to the hospital?
When to have a vaginal exam?
Lighting in the room?
Use of electronic monitoring of your labor?
Whether or when to have a cesarean?
Whether or not to have an episiotomy?
Whether or not to have your labor induced?

Whether or not to film the birth or take photos?
How many medical staff will be in the room?
Who gets to announce the sex of the baby?
Where you give birth? Home? Hospital? Birthing center?
Who receives (catches) the baby?
How does the mother breathe as the baby descends and emerges?
Who and when the umbilical cord is cut?
How is the placenta birthed?
Does the baby have its nose and mouth routinely suctioned?
What are the vaccines, and when are they given?
Breastfeeding or not?
Rooming in with baby or not?

There are different approaches to maternity care providers. Some are in the active management range, and others are in the expectant management field. Choosing which is best for you and sorting which care providers match your style should be done with due diligence. The more options you choose for the doctor to make among the choices on the list, the more you would prefer an active management–style approach. The more options on the list you choose for you and your partner to make, the more you would prefer an expectant management–style approach.

Active	Expectant
Set Menu What is done to every woman: • Regular ultra-sounds throughout pregnancy. • Vaginal exams during pregnancy. • Stretch and sweep at forty weeks. • Routine inductions. • Episiotomies.	A la Carte • Care provider believes birth is a normal physiological event. • If the mom and baby are well, then take a wait and see approach. • Have lower cesarean rates. • Do not do episiotomies. • No vaginal exams during pregnancy. • Wait for labor to start spontaneously.
Of the opinion that is it better to do something "just in case" to avoid something going wrong.	Of the opinion that "if it ain't broke, don't fix it."

Designed by grmarc/Freepik. Photo courtesy of ParentLink.

Which photo depicts how you see yourself giving birth?

Ensuring that your choice of care providers matches your belief system is key to having the experience you desire. Here is a grid to help illustrate the differences:

1 normal

2
3
4
5
6
7
8
9 requires medical intervention
10 Extreme

Where does your care provider fall on the grid? Are they comfortable only to seven? Where are you on the grid? Do you want to wait until nine and then intervene, or are you more comfortable with an intervention at eight? Make sure you and your care provider are on the same page.

Earlier in the book, I listed questions to ask care providers to ascertain if they will support natural birth. It's essential to understand first the hormones of labor. Here are the questions again, with why you would ask them.

How do you feel about me laboring and birthing off the bed?

Women need to feel uninhibited for labor to progress smoothly. Movement can facilitate shorter labor, more comfort for the mother, and an easier descent for the baby.

How long are you comfortable for me to labor?

Each woman and baby work together through labor and birth. Each labor is unique. As long as the mother and baby are doing fine, why is it necessary to intervene due to a preconceived idea that labor has a time limit?

When do you find it necessary to induce labor?

Full term is anywhere between thirty-seven to forty-two weeks. That's a five-week span. Only 5 percent of women give birth at forty weeks. The average is forty-one weeks plus three days. As long as the mother and baby are fine, why is it necessary to intervene?

How do you feel about my eating and drinking during labor?

Imagine if you were on an all-day hike with no food or water. Women are not ill. They need to eat and drink during labor. Muscles do not perform properly when dehydrated. The uterus is a muscle that is working. And what is impressive is that this muscle is part of our ANS (autonomic nervous system). It works without our conscious effort. And how odd is it that this set of muscles is the only one in the human body that is considered painful when functioning normally? All our body functions are designed to work without peril or pain.

How do you feel about me having a doula at the birth?

If not, why not? A doula does not interfere with medical protocols. She is there for informational and emotional support only. Since love hormones are involved during labor, women need to have continuity of care, enabling them to feel safe and loved.

What is your cesarean rate?

WHO states that between 10 percent to 15 percent of all births require caesareans. The USA has a national average of 32 percent.

Dr. Lorne Campbell, a strong proponent of HypnoBirthing and family practitioner in New York, performs one cesarean a year. It is mainly his trust in women's bodies and their ability to birth their babies if they are only patient. His advice to maternity care providers? Put your hands in your pockets and watch how amazing the woman's birthing body knows what to do.

https://www.youtube.com/watch?v=RNmDAm9msog

Your doctor's cesarean rate will let you know your odds of receiving a C-section with this care provider. And remember my story earlier about Dr. Park in South Korea? Her cesarean rates went from 15 to 7 percent in one month after her midwives received HypnoBirthing training. She updated me later that it went down to 5 percent after the midwives changed to working on shifts rather than with only one woman. As the midwife tired, she felt the need to intervene to speed things up. As the midwife's energy drained, the laboring mother could feel this and respond accordingly. I always had a backup doula in case I tired; my energy would then be wrong for labor to progress.

CHOOSING YOUR BIRTH LOCATION

Depending on where you are, there are choices for where to give birth. Home is probably where you would be most comfortable. We'll talk about the hormones in labor, which will explain why home would be most comfortable. Many midwives will attend home births and are happy to accommodate your birth plan. Some mothers opt for a free birth—to have no maternity care provider present.

Activity 3

A birthing center might be an option for you, or you might prefer a hospital setting. For these options, here is a chart you can create for each hospital / birthing center you visit for comparison.

Hospital or Birth Center Comparison	Option 1	Option 2	Option 3	Option 4
Labor pool in room				
Water births				
Showers in labor room				
Birth stool available				
Birth ball available				
Microwave in room				
Dim lamps in room				
Thermostat in room				
Foam floor mats				
CD players in room				
Electric aromatherapy available				
Natural light in room				
Works with doulas				
Staff trained to support HypnoBirthing®				
Neonatal intensive care				
Kangaroo care				
Wireless monitoring				
Mandatory baby visit to nursery				
Number of birthing suites				
Average number of births per day				
Public or private				
Average cost normal birth private room				
Cesarean rates				
Other key points				

Now why these options might be relevant to you:

Labor Pool in Room

Water can provide deep relaxation and ease the discomfort that might be felt. Women tend to feel an invisible wall is around them, providing the privacy they need for labor to progress more smoothly. It provides ease of movement with buoyancy.

Water Births

It is the same as laboring in a pool plus the added benefit of the warmth, and the water reduces the risk of the perineum tearing.

Showers in Labor Room

The water is relaxing and provides direct pressure on the sacrum as needed.

Birth Stool Available

Most Westerners have lost the squatting ability for any length of time. Squatting opens the pelvis an additional 30 percent. This plus the force of gravity helps the baby descend. Squatting also shortens the distance the baby needs to move from the cervix to the vaginal opening.

Birth Ball Available

The hips' movement whilst rotating on the birth ball aids in the baby descending through the pelvic inlet. The buoyancy of the ball provides easy movement. It can be used in many ways to facilitate movement during labor, including your birthing companion.

Microwave in Room

Facilitates the heating of rice socks for placement where needed.

Dim Lamps in Room

Provides the ability for deep relaxation and the intimacy for labor to progress smoothly and calmly.

Thermostat in Room

As labor progresses, some women feel a transition between hot and cold. Being able to control the temperature provides laboring mothers the comfort they deserve. When the baby is born, they are coming from a warm, wet environment. A thermostat will allow you to keep the room at a welcoming temperature for the baby.

Foam Floor Mats

Many mothers find that laboring on their knees and rocking their hips is a comfort. Foam floor mats provide comfort to the mother.

CD Players in Room

Music can produce endorphins in the mother, facilitating the progress of labor.

Electric Aromatherapy Available

Aromatherapy can produce endorphins in the mother, facilitating the progress of labor.

Natural Light in Room

Windows with a view can be a comfort to a mother versus the harsh lighting of fluorescents.

Works with Doulas

The parents might decide they want to have a doula to support them through pregnancy, labor, birth, and early days.

Staff Trained to Support HypnoBirthing®

If the parents opt for HypnoBirthing classes, it would be easier if the maternity care providers understand the language and premise of HypnoBirthing.

Neonatal Intensive Care

Is there a NICU on-site with proximity to the labor room?

Kangaroo Care

Does the facility promote kangaroo care with newborns and premature babies?

Wireless Monitoring

If monitoring is required, does the facility provide wireless monitoring so as not to inhibit movement?

Mandatory Baby Visit to Nursery

Does the facility require the baby to visit the nursery before rooming in with the parents?

Family Bed

Does the facility provide a family bed so the parents can sleep together and a trundle bed for the older sibling?

Number of Birthing Suites and Average Number of Births per Day

It's important to know if there are enough rooms available and to ascertain if the number of births per day would motivate the staff to move you through quickly in order to free up a room for another laboring mother entering the facility.

Public or Private

Is the facility public or private organization?

Average Cost for a Normal Birth Private Room

It is always good to know, especially if you don't have insurance coverage.

Cesarean Rates

This is useful for comparing the hospitals' ability to support natural birth options and to sort your odds of having a natural birth.

Other Key Points

What else is important to you?

NUTRITION, EXERCISE, AND MENTAL APPROACH

There are some essential cornerstones of a healthy pregnancy: labor, birth, and baby. Nutrition, exercise, and mental approach play key roles in childbirth.

First, it's important to remember the importance of oral care. Gum infections enter your bloodstream and might cause preterm labor.

For a woman with an average BMI before pregnancy, it is desirable to consume 2,000 calories a day of nutritious foods and take a moderate-dose vitamin and mineral supplement that includes at least 400 mcg of folic acid and at least 18 mg of iron. This is for an average woman with average dietary needs. Having a well-balanced diet can reduce your risk for many of the complications that are sometimes experienced in pregnancy. If you have any questions regarding your dietary needs, please seek the advice of a certified nutritionist.

Some of the potential complications that can be remedied but not limited to the following:

Assist in the Proper Implementation of the Egg

Fruits and vegetables that include vitamin C help form connective tissue; breads and cereals, eggs, and milk are a few good sources. Trace minerals, such as copper, help prevent birth defects (fruits and vegetables). Calcium helps build strong bones (calcium-rich foods include dairy and green leafy vegetables).

Reduce Early Pregnancy Fatigue

B vitamins (found in grains) help convert calories into energy and promote healthy growth and development.

Reduce Morning Sickness

A study from Harvard Medical School in Boston found that women who consumed diets high in saturated fats from dairy foods and meat during the months before they conceived were more likely to suffer from morning sickness. Try eating smaller meals more often. Try not to have an empty stomach. Ginger and mint teas sometimes help relieve nausea, as does soda crackers or ginger cookies.

Assist in Avoiding Constipation

Foods high in fiber help you to keep regular. High-fiber foods are carrots, apples, pears, oatmeal, whole wheat toast, and whole grain bagels.

Reduce the risk of preterm labor, hypertension, preeclampsia, and gestational diabetes.

Folic acid prevents preterm labor in the last trimester. Iron helps prevent preterm delivery. Good sources of iron are extra-lean meat, fish, poultry, cooked beans, and peas. Chromium (found in whole grains) might reduce pregnancy-induced gestational diabetes. Vitamin C helps support connective tissue, the most abundant tissue in the body and the glue that holds all other tissues together, aiding in normal cell division and in the formation of skin and all the linings in the body, from the lungs and bladder to the blood vessels. Folic acid prevents neural tube defects in the early stages of pregnancy.

Minimize the Risks of Malformations

Folic acid prevents neural tube defects in the early stages of pregnancy. Wheat germ, brewer's yeast, and oats are a few sources of folic acid. Vitamin B_6 is essential in developing your baby's nervous system, the formation of all tissues, and protein metabolism. Yeast, whole grain wheat germ, and orange juice are good sources of chromium. Calcium might help to prevent pregnancy-induced high blood pressure. Low-fat milk products, sardines, canned salmon with bones, and tofu are a few sources.

Assist in Easing the Birthing Process

Magnesium maintains uterine relaxation during pregnancy and aids in contraction during labor. Good sources are low-fat milk, peanuts, bananas, wheat germ, and whole grains.

Super Foods for Pregnancy

Spinach, kidney beans, strawberries, tofu, wheat germ, broccoli, papaya, salmon, nonfat milk, and water.

Healthy Snacks Suggestions

Whole wheat pita dunked in hummus and topped with sliced red peppers.

Tomato soup made with nut-based milk and topped with cilantro.

Asparagus spears lightly sautéed in chicken broth and garlic, then cooled for a crunchy snack.

A sweet potato, sliced into strips and baked until crispy.

Pitted lemon-flavored dried plums with an almond stuffed into each.

Cantaloupe cubes drizzled with lime juice.

A handful of raw chocolate morsels, dried cranberries, and almonds.

Tom Brewer, a doctor who wrote a book on pregnancy nutrition, suggests drinking lots of water. The amniotic fluid is replacing itself three times a day (averaging one cup an hour), and the mother's kidneys are filtering the baby's waste. Dehydration can cause preterm labor.

It is not necessary to stress about your nutrition. By eating a variety of nutritious foods, you should be well on your way to a balanced diet. We encourage you to read further and happy eating! If you do splurge, eat it with joy, not guilt. It is not beneficial to eat guilt.

Nutrition Resources
Books

Roberts, Holly. *Your Vegetarian Pregnancy: A Month-by-Month Guide to Health and Nutrition.* Available at www.half.com, $5.99 + shipping.

Somer, Elizabeth. *Nutrition for a Healthy Pregnancy.*

Ward, Elizabeth. *Pregnancy Nutrition, Good Health for You and Your Baby.* Available at www.half.com.

Website

http://nutrition.birthingnaturally.net/brewerslideshow/brewerdiet_files/frame.htm

Women gain weight during pregnancy, and there are fat stores for a reason. Women during labor do not eat much whilst their body is working. After the baby is born, the baby will be feeding, on average, every two hours. Those fat stores will aid the mother through this time of challenges.

Components of Weight Gain

Developing baby	3.5 kg
Placenta	0.6 kg
Amniotic fluid	1 kg
Extra breast tissue	0.5 kg
Extra blood	1.2 kg
Fluid	1.2 kg
Uterus	1 kg
Fat stores	2–4 kg
Total weight gain	10–13 kg

BMI Prepregnancy	Preferred Weight Gain
Below 19.8	28–40 lbs or 13–18 kg
19.9–26	25–34 lbs or 12–16 kg
26.1–29	15–25 lbs or 7–11 kg
29.1 and above	15 lbs or 11 kg

The following vitamin and mineral charts indicate the functions/deficiency and signs / good sources. Many women believe that leg cramps are common during late pregnancy. This is how the body is indicating it is low on calcium or magnesium.

Vitamins	Functions	Deficiency Signs	Good Sources
Vitamin A	Promotes healthy eyes, skin, and hair and also maintains the mucous membranes of the nose, throat, lungs, and gut.	Eye, skin, and hair problems; poor night vision; impaired bone growth; and increased susceptibility to infections.	Eggs, dairy foods, butter, margarine, liver, kidneys, and fish liver oil.
Beta carotene	Improves immunity.	Increased susceptibility to infections.	Yellow, green, orange, and red vegetables and fruit.
Vitamin B group (eight vitamins)	Needed for the processes that release the energy in carbohydrates, fats, and proteins consumed in the diet. Also needed for the nervous system, formation for red blood cells, healthy skin, and heart.	Fatigue, nerve problems, decreased ability to cope with stress, depression, and skin problems.	Yeast, whole grain breads and cereals, legumes, eggs milk, nuts, green leafy vegetables, liver, kidneys, meat, poultry, fish, seafood, and fortified breakfast cereals.
Folate (a B-group vitamin)	Essential for DNA synthesis, protein synthesis, and red blood cell production.	Anemia. A low intake prior to conception and during pregnancy can increase the risk of spinal tube defects in the baby.	Brewer's yeast, wheat germ, bran, green leafy vegetables, avocados, oats, liver, tomatoes, organs, and melons.

Vitamins	Functions	Deficiency Signs	Good Sources
Vitamin B12	Works with folate. Essential for the functioning of all cells and protein, fat and carbohydrate metabolism, as well as healthy nerves.	Anemia, nervous system disorders, depression, and poor memory.	Only found in animal foods: dairy products, organ meats, eggs, red meat, and seafood. Vegans may need to take a supplement.
Vitamin C	Needed for healthy skin, bones, cartilage, and teeth. Helps the body to absorb iron and helps protect against infections and chronic diseases.	Tissue breakdown, easy bleeding and bruising, and fatigue.	Fruit and vegetables: capsicum, guava, Brussels sprouts, pawpaw, kiwi, melon, mangoes, citrus, berries, broccoli, pineapple, and cabbage.
Vitamin D	Needed to absorb calcium for healthy bones and teeth. Sunlight also helps the body make its own Vitamin D. Needed to make hormones.	Muscle and bone weakness. Rickets in children	Egg yolk, cheese, margarine, milk, vegetables oils, oily fish, and liver.
Vitamin E	Needed for healthy blood vessels and tissues, including the heart. Works with other antioxidant vitamins and minerals to protect against disease.	Deficiency is rare. Prevents normal growth.	Egg yolks, nuts, seeds, whole grain cereals, wheat germ, vegetable oils and margarine, meat, and peanut butter.
Vitamin K	Needed for the normal clotting of blood. Essential for the formation of protein substances in the bones and kidneys.	Nosebleeds and excessive bleeding.	Broccoli, lettuce cabbage, spinach, cauliflower, legumes, and liver.

Minerals	Functions	Deficiency Signs	Good Sources
Calcium	Essential for strong bones and teeth. Regulates nerve and muscle function and may help reduce high blood pressure.	Rickets, osteoporosis, cramps, muscle problems, high blood pressure, and heart arrhythmias.	Dairy products, almonds, brewer's yeast, dried figs, salmon and its bones, sardines, tahini, calcium-enriched soy milk, and tofu.
Iodine	Needed for thyroid hormone production, regulation of metabolic rate, proper growth, sex hormones, healthy skin, nails, hair, and teeth.	Goiter, hypothyroidism, bulging eyes, low libido, brittle nails, fatigue, weight gain, and constipation.	Iodized salt, kelp, clams, shrimp, haddock, oysters, salmon, sardines, cheddar, pineapple, and onions.
Iron	Needed to make hemoglobin (the compound in red blood cells allowing them to carry oxygen) and myoglobin (the oxygen-carrying compound in muscles).	A relatively common deficiency. Fatigue, poor circulation, anemia, depression, less able to concentrate, and decreased physical and mental performance.	Red meats are the richest source; liver, chicken, turkey, and fish are not as rich. Whole grain bread, legumes, dark-green leafy vegetables, eggs, nuts, apricots, and sunflower seeds.
Magnesium	Essential for the proper function of nerves and muscles, including the heart.	Weakness, fatigue, anxiety, agitation, confusion, muscle tremors, cramps, convulsions, and heart rhythm disturbances.	Whole grain cereal products, wheat germ, brewer's yeast, almonds, molasses, seafood, kelp, green leafy vegetables, nuts, and legumes.

Minerals	Functions	Deficiency Signs	Good Sources
Phosphorus	Essential for healthy bones and teeth. Helps with nutrient absorption, energy production, nerve transmission, metabolism, and muscle contraction.	Deficiency is rare. Anxiety, fatigue, muscle weakness, bone pains, osteoporosis, and rickets.	Dairy products, eggs, whole grains, legumes, garlic, nuts, and seeds.
Potassium	Essential for the normal functioning of nerves and muscles; promotes normal blood pressure and heartbeat.	Fatigue, heart disturbances, and extreme thirst.	Vegetables, fruit, avocados, whole grain cereals, seeds, dates, raisins, nuts, and potatoes.
Selenium	Works together with vitamin E to prevent or inhibit the damaging effects of antioxidants.	Premature aging, muscle degeneration, and liver disease.	Butter, wheat germ, barley, whole wheat bread, garlic, Brazil nuts, and cider vinegar.
Sodium	Needed for nerve and muscle functions and regulating the balance of fluid in the body.	Deficiency is rare. Dehydration, vomiting, and cramps.	Kale, yeast extract, salted nuts, bread, cheese, and margarine.
Zinc	Needed for healthy eyes and skin; improves immunity. Essential for taste, smell, appetite, and carbohydrate metabolism. Important for wound healing, normal growth, reproduction, and development.	Decreased fertility and libido, poor sense of taste and smell, poor wound healing, less energy, and less resistance to infections.	Red meat, eggs, seafood, yeast, milk, whole grain cereals, liver, cheese, yoghurt, green leafy vegetables, chicken, oats, and legumes.

References

Healthy Eating. Periplus Editions. 2001.
Somer, Elizabeth. *Nutrition for a Healthy Pregnancy*.
www.something-fishy.org/dangers/vitamins.php

Activity 4
Nutrition Exercise

Take a week's time to take stock of your nutritional intake. At the end of a week, you should be able to see where you need to make corrections. This chart is for an average woman with average dietary needs. Do seek the advice of a naturopath to fine-tune your diet.

	Serving Equivalents	Your Servings	Required Servings	+ or –	Action Plan
Calcium-rich foods	1 cup of milk or 226 ml yogurt or fortified soy milk 1 oz or 28 g cheese		two		
Fruits and veggies	1 piece fresh ½ cup or 120 ml cooked		six to nine		
Protein	3 oz meat or 85 g 1 cup or 236 g beans 8 oz or 226 g of tofu		two		
Grains	½ cup or 97 g rice 1 slice bread		six		
Quenchers	8 oz or 226 ml		eight		

Other sources of calcium-rich foods easier for your body to utilize:

Sesame seeds. A quarter cup of sesame seeds has 351 mg calcium.
Spinach. A cup of boiled spinach has 245 mg.
Collard greens. A cup of boiled collard greens has 266 mg.
Blackstrap molasses. 1 tbsp has about 137 mg.
Kelp. A cup of raw kelp has 136 mg.
Tahini. 2 tbsp of raw tahini.
Broccoli. 2 cups of boiled broccoli have 124 mg.
Swiss chard. A cup of boiled chard has 102 mg.
Kale. A cup of boiled kale has 94 mg.
Brazil nuts. 2 ounces of Brazil nuts have 90 mg.
Celery. 2 cups of raw celery have 81 mg.
Almonds. An ounce of almonds (twenty-three nuts) has 75 mg.

EXERCISE

Exercise is also a cornerstone of a healthy pregnancy, baby, labor, and birth. It helps us throughout our lives to remain healthy. It's easy when we're caught up in the everyday work, clean, shop, and cook mode to leave out taking care of ourselves and our bodies. Consider putting it on your calendar so that you exercise daily, even if just for twenty minutes. A previous student of mine and friend in Singapore co-started a gym called Ritual. Their premise was to make it a ritual to work out for twenty minutes every day. Their exercise regimen worked most fantastically for Oli Pettigrew. He is a TV personality and former model. He was challenged to see the transformation in just eight weeks. He went from handsome modeling man to a hunk with washboard abs. One hour a week will usually fit into everyone's routine, so no excuses! Recruit your partner to participate or at least encourage you on your road to health!

Encouraging words from Oli:

Achieving my goals always seemed insurmountable when it came to exercise—that's when I just started listening to people who knew more than me. People always talk about not having the "time" for their fitness, but the ease and efficiency of something like 'Ritual' take that argument

> and do burpees all over its face. Three training sessions in a week is 60 minutes of exercise—an hour. We can all find an hour. It's important to let yourself be a priority. Invest in yourself now so you can cash it in later. Seven years later, and I still train efficiently, I still eat well, and I still feel great. My ritual became a habit. That habit became a lifestyle. Now, I know what you're thinking, it's easy for some former model to say that. The significant part of training like we do at Ritual is that it's open to everyone and every fitness level. I'll be on the training floor with men and women, from teenagers to retirees, at all fitness levels. It's about finding your own limits and pushing on through. Anyone can find their fitness. Anyone. You just have to start! One step at a time — before you know it, you'll discover YOUR ritual. (Oli Pettigrew)

And you might be lucky enough to live near a Ritual gym; you can find them here: https://www.ritualgym.com/en-gb/locations.

As a doula supporting moms who were avidly into yoga, I found that their labors were shorter in duration and much more comfortable. The practice of breath work with movement dovetails with the progression of labor. Other great options are walking, swimming, hiking, dancing, Pilates, and weight training. If you are already pregnant, do not overdo it. It is not time to build muscle but to maintain it. Pregnancy is a beautiful time to get in touch with your body; learn all its subtle cues. If you are tired, take a break. If you are hungry, eat a healthy snack. We are taught at a very early stage in life to ignore our body's cues. We learn to ignore at school when we are hungry as lunch is scheduled at twelve; when we need to wee, we must wait for the break. This is a great time to be primal, as being primal will be needed during labor.

Pelvic floor exercises are key to a more comfortable birth and reduce the risk of perineum tearing. Imagine, if you will, trying to hold in your urine or not pass wind. These are your pelvic floor muscles engaging. You want to tighten and relax these muscles daily throughout your life. You can factor in a trigger to remember to do them. Consider that you do your pelvic floors every time you brush your teeth. During labor, this is important because as the baby descends, you need your pelvic floor relaxed, not taut. It is an easier descent for the baby and reduces your risk of tearing. The added bonus is that you reduce the chance at an older age of weeing for women when you sneeze. Recent studies show that it reduces the risk of needing Viagra and minimizes prostate problems for men.

Six to eight weeks before your guess date, massage the perineum every day for five minutes. This is the area between your vaginal opening and anus. Massaging this area routinely will reduce your risk of tearing. It improves the birthing region's blood supply and health, increases elasticity in the perineal folds, acquaints you with tissues, and relaxes the sphincter that needs to be relaxed as the baby is birthed. Virgin olive oil, almond oil, apricot oil, or a lubricating gel can be used as long as there are no perfumes or dyes. If the mother has a challenge reaching the perineum as the baby bump grows, the birthing companion can gently and respectfully assist.

A mother's posture is important during pregnancy as well. Proper sitting and standing will help the baby fit into the pelvic inlet as pregnancy progresses, facilitating an easier descent for the baby. Sitting on a Pilates ball aids in the proper sitting posture.

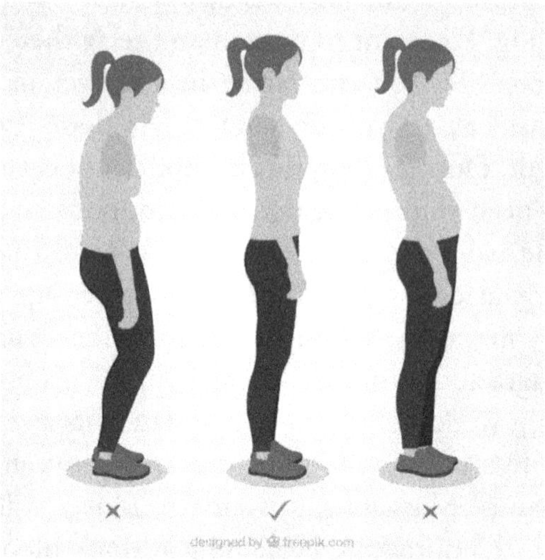

<a href="https://www.freepik.com/free-photos-vectors/woman">Woman vector created by freepik - www.freepik.com</a>

<a href="https://www.freepik.com/free-photos-vectors/hand">Hand vector created by freepik - www.freepik.com</a>

MENTAL APPROACH

How we view pregnancy, labor, and birth will affect our pregnancy and birth experience. We reviewed our beliefs at the beginning of this section. I intend to encourage you to view the normality of our reproductive system and our innate knowledge of how to birth and dispel so many stifling myths out there. Birth is a normal physiological event. One a woman's body is designed to do. Our reproductive system is part of our automatic nervous system. Just as we don't focus on breathing, heart beating, and food digesting, our reproductive system functions beyond our conscious control. We have been brainwashed by our parents, peers, medical community, and the media that birth is traumatic and dramatic. It doesn't have to be either.

Hormones of Labor

Understanding the hormones of labor will erase all the misconceptions about what is needed for labor to progress efficiently and smoothly.

Oxytocin is a love hormone. It is what causes the surges of labor in a woman's body. It is the same hormone our body releases when making love. Basically, the same energy that gets the baby in there gets the baby out. According to Dr. Michel Odent in *The Functions of the Orgasm* (I highly recommend reading his book), these inhibit oxytocin production:

- observation
- being cold
- fear
- feeling inhibited

So basically, everything in most hospital-based births inhibits the progress of labor. Women need privacy, warmth, comfortable surroundings, and the feeling of being safe enough to allow their body to dictate their behavior. As labor progresses, women make noise. They move in sensual ways. Women need to feel like they can do this without anyone intruding or intimidating.

Endorphins are our feel-good hormones and control the discomfort of labor. Endorphins can be encouraged with the following:

Breath work
Massage
Chocolate
Music
Aroma
Humor
Movement
Hypnosis

As the body surges during labor, oxytocin builds up to a peak, endorphins match it, and the surge descends.

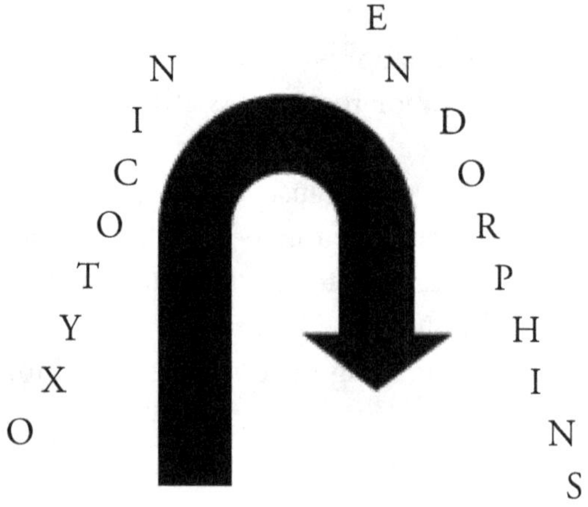

Fear causes the body to constrict rather than relax, creating the majority of the discomfort during labor. Learning to trust in the body and its ability to labor and birth easily and comfortably will facilitate a more comfortable, quick birthing. When the body is flooded with oxytocin and endorphins, adrenaline is reduced or restricted. The comfort is not only easier for the mother. The baby as well, if being monitored, will show a calmer tracing.

NORMAL PHYSIOLOGY OF LABOR

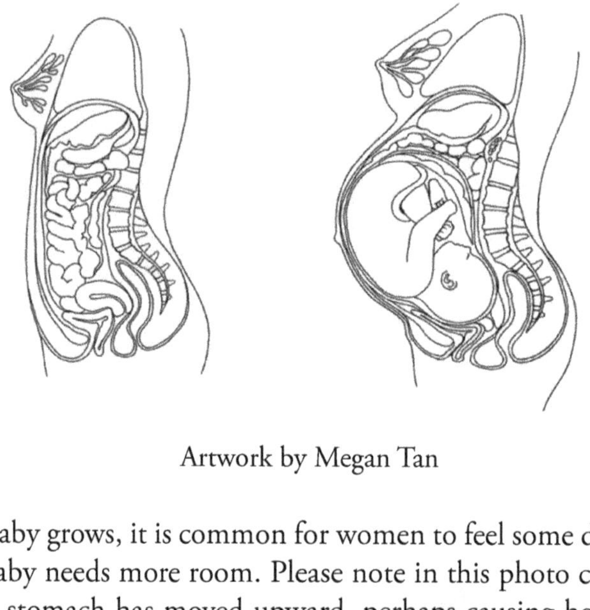

Artwork by Megan Tan

As the baby grows, it is common for women to feel some discomfort, as the baby needs more room. Please note in this photo comparison that the stomach has moved upward, perhaps causing heartburn or the feeling of fullness after a snack. Notice how the bladder flattened out. It is common for women to feel the need to urinate only to find a simple trickle with no pressure relief. Note also how the vagina is next to the rectum. As the baby descends, there will be pressure on the rectum. Any waste in the rectum will be ejected. The pressure on the rectum will feel like the most urgent need to poo. Your body will take over and begin to move the baby down and out. Dr. Michel Odent calls this the natural expulsive reflex.

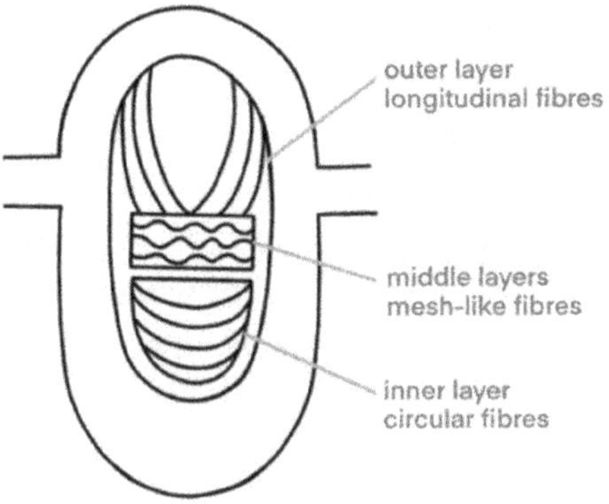

Artwork by Megan Tan

There are three layers of muscles to the uterus. The outer layer consists of longitudinal muscles that are more fibrous at the top. The middle layer consists of connective tissues. The innermost layer consists of horizontal muscles that are more fibrous at the bottom of the cervix. According to Dr. Grantly Dick Read in *Childbirth Without Fear*, all our body functions are designed to work without peril or pain. The uterine muscles are the only muscles in the human body that are considered painful when functioning properly.

The outer layer, during a surge, will push downward. The inner layer will pull the cervix up, open it, and expand upward, causing the abdomen to rise to a peak.

Here is a link to a woman posting photos of her baby bump during and after a surge: https://community.whattoexpect.com/forums/june-2014-babies/topic/contractions-make-my-belly-contort.html.

The baby's head applies pressure on the cervix, and along with the production of hormones, the cervix opens. There is much talk about the magic of 10 cm, so a great visualization for you is the following: 1 cm is a blueberry, 5 cm is a lime, and 10 cm is a bagel.

During labor, the baby descends in a spiral-like clockwise movement with the baby rotating in a clockwise fashion through the pelvis. The pelvis is oval-shaped, and the baby descends with the head facing your hip and then turns to allow the shoulders through, facing the bum. The baby's head has bony plates that have not fused and enable the head to compress and fit through the pelvis. Many women instinctively rotate their hips during labor. Here is a video to observe this descent: https://www.youtube.com/watch?v=ze53Ep-gwBQ.

The pelvis is fused with cartilage in the front, allowing expansion as the baby moves downward. One of the comfort measures I provided as a doula during the labor was to apply pressure against the hip bones on each side of the pelvic inlet with every surge. This technique allowed the pelvis to expand at the pelvic outlet. The hormones released in a woman's body prepare her for labor by softening the cartilage, ligaments, and bones for expansion; smoothing the walls of the vagina for an easier descent; and increasing vaginal discharge. Many women start to waddle walk at the end of their pregnancy as their hip joints have loosened to prepare for labor.

Positioning during labor will also aid the ease of progress for mother and baby. Mostly, it is intuitive; if the mother can tune into what her body wants, what her baby wants, she can facilitate the labor.

*Birth Move*Ment* is a fantastic film that shows how different positions during labor facilitate birthing. On the following pages are examples of different positions in which to labor.

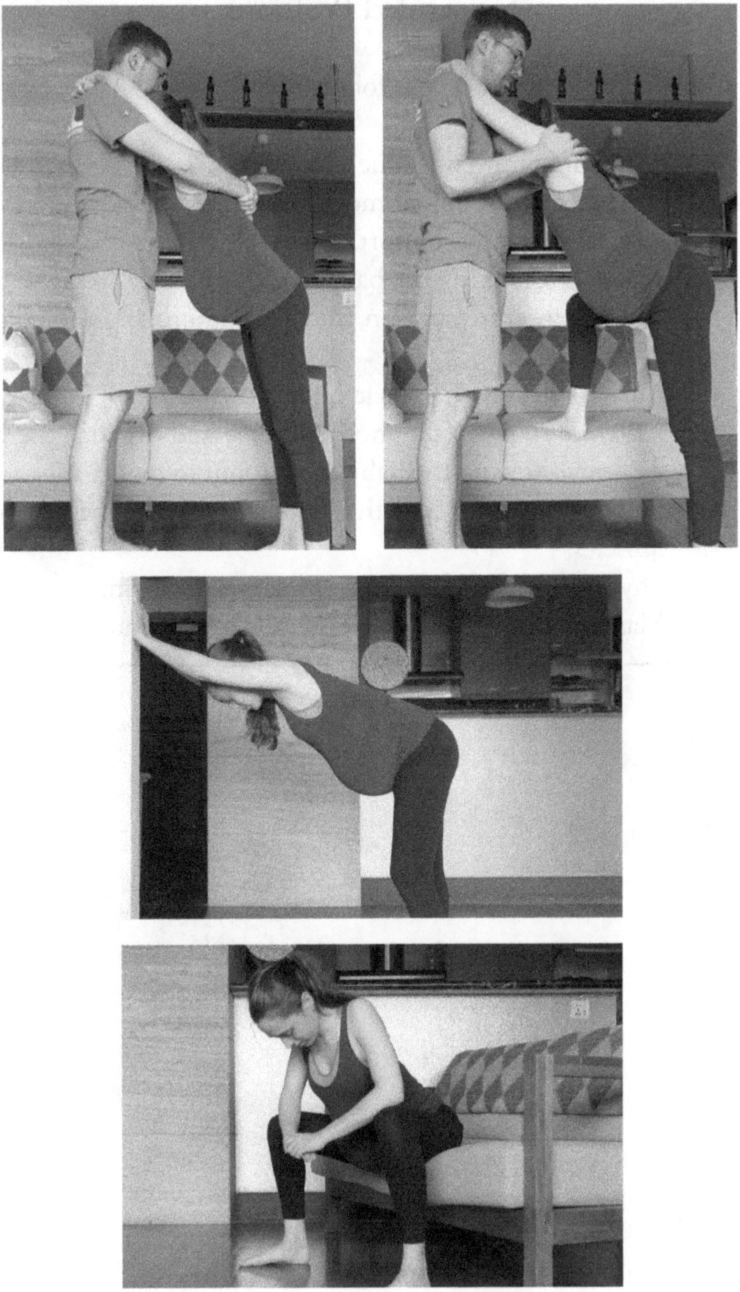

Photos courtesy of Thomas Weinmeyer

Suspended Positions

These positions will do the following:

- Stimulate or intensify the surges.
- Encourage the baby to move lower into the pelvis.
- Alleviate back discomfort.
- Assist in realigning the baby's head.
- Create more pressure on the pelvis improving the quality of the surges.
- Aids in relaxing the pelvic floor muscles.
- Increases room in the mother's torso and expands the pelvic area, allowing the baby more room to maneuver.
- Full foot contact on the floor relaxes the pelvic floor muscles.
- Physical contact with partner releases oxytocin.
- Massage, music, and aromatherapy release endorphins.

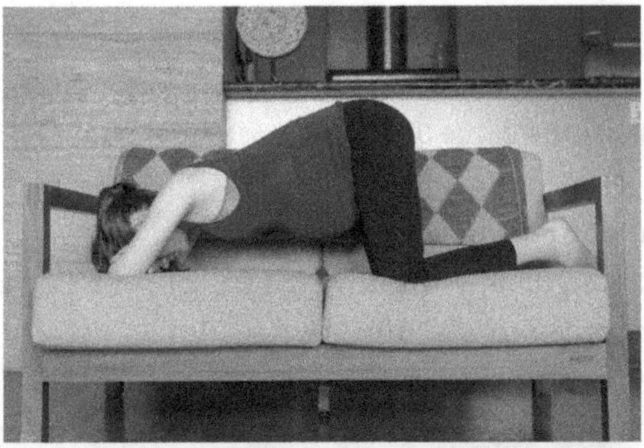
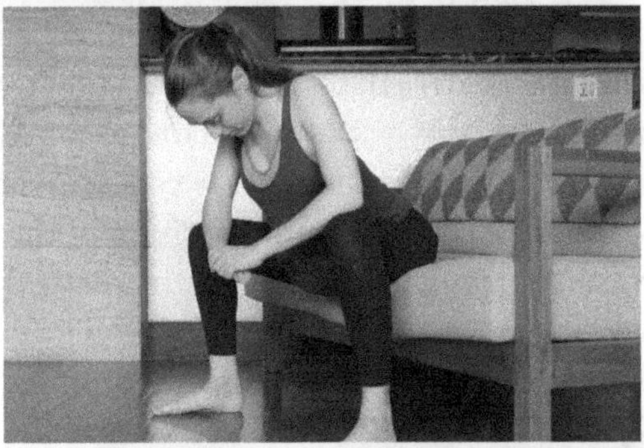

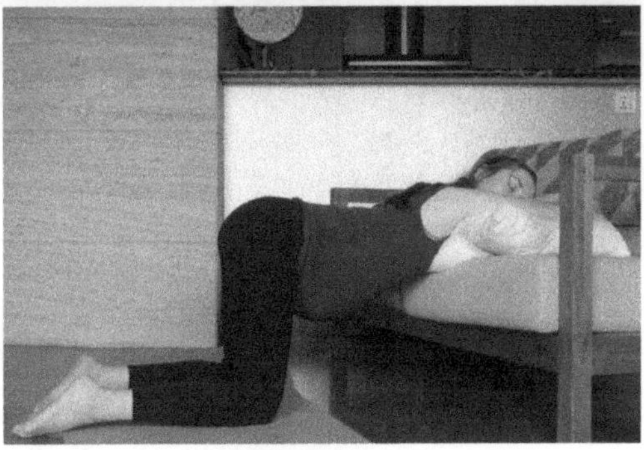

Forward Leaning

These positions can do the following:

- Stimulate or increase surges.
- Encourage baby to move lower into the pelvis.
- Alleviate back discomfort.
- Gravity and movement can provoke a.
- Helps the body and pelvic floor muscles relax.
- Hanging suspended by a rope or from partner's shoulders loosens the maternal torso and expands the pelvic area, providing the baby with more room to move and rotate.
- In addition, good full foot-floor contact relaxes the pelvic floor muscles, optimizing the position of the baby.
- Physical contact with the partner increases the production of oxytocin.
- Music and aromatherapy release endorphins.

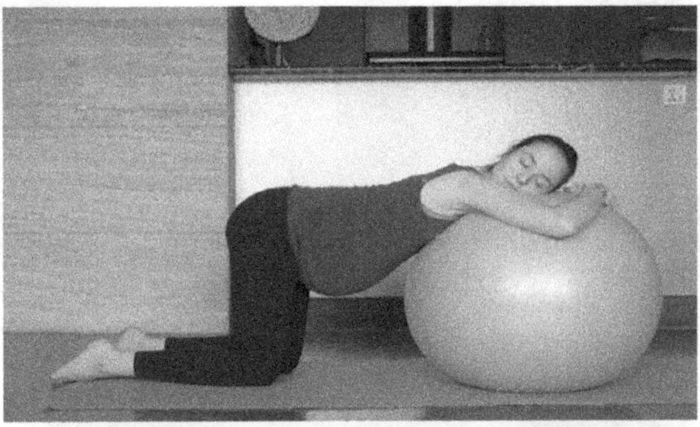

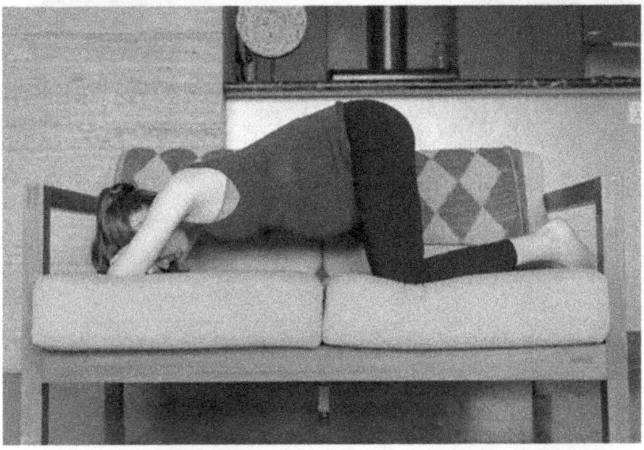

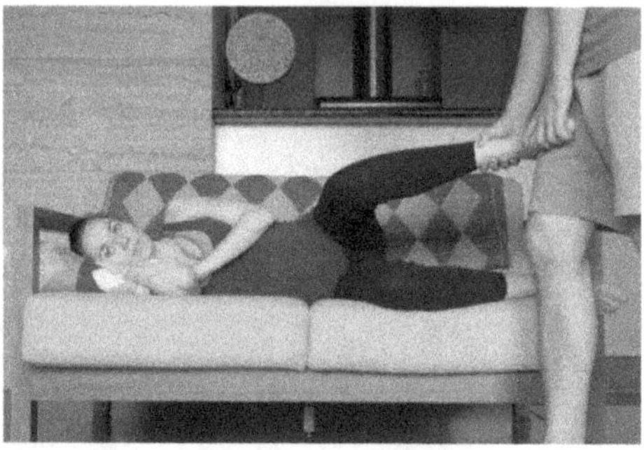

Asymmetrical Positions

- When the baby's head does not engage.
- When there is back discomfort.
- Changes the shape of the pelvic inlet, allowing the baby to descend properly.
- When the mother is tiring or labor is progressing too quickly.
- Lying on the side where the baby's back is facilitates baby moving into the pelvic inlet.
- Music, aromatherapy, and dim lights increase the production of endorphins.
- Physical contact with partner increases the production of oxytocin.

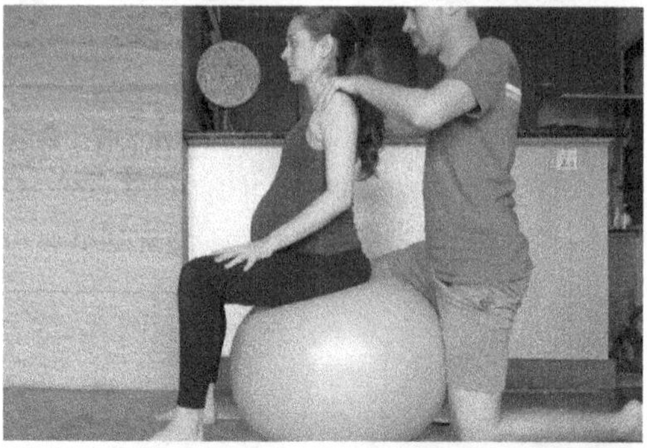

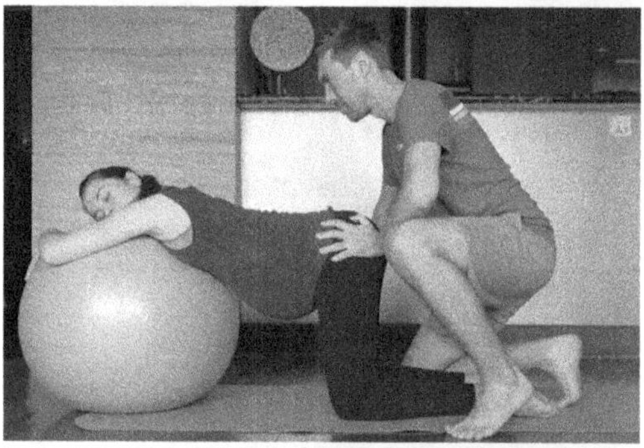

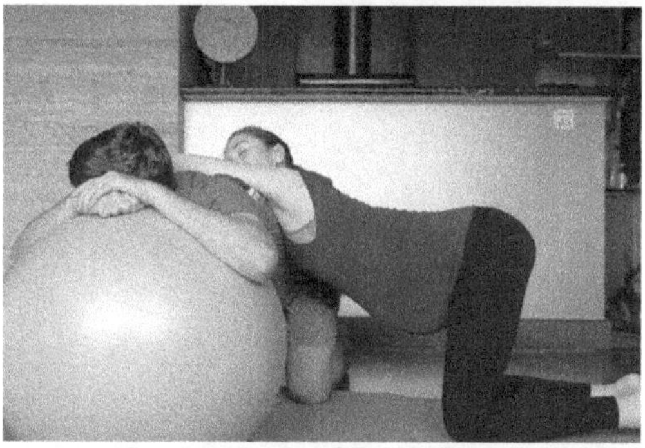

SITTING POSITIONS

These positions are useful:

- If mother is tired.
- After an epidural.
- Encourages the baby to move lower into the pelvis.
- Speeds labor up.
- Increases room for the baby's head to emerge.
- Provides optimal pelvic mobility.
- These positions take advantage of gravity.
- Facilitates gentle spontaneous pushing.
- Increases efficiency of the surges.
- Enlarges the pelvic outlet.
- Full foot-floor contact relaxes the pelvic floor.
- Physical contact with partner releases oxytocin.
- Massage releases endorphins.
- Pressure on the hips increases the pelvic outlet opening.
- Music and aromatherapy releases endorphins.

The important thing to remember is that your body will tell you what position you should be in if you tune in and pay attention. There is no way to know ahead of time what will suit you and the baby best. Just know there are a lot of options.

BIRTH PLAN POINTERS

If you are planning a home birth, your birth plan is simple. Discuss it with your partner, midwife, and doula; and you're good to go.

If you are planning a birth center birth, it's also simple. Ask what their policies and protocols are, and you're good to go.

Hospital births are a bit more complicated.

It's important to know what you are asking for when you list it on your birth plan. I'm not a big advocate of checklist items, as creating your plan requires you to think about each item and why you want it. Main points to consider:

Inductions

Every intervention has a decisive impact on how the labor progresses. Consider that as long as the mother and baby are okay, leave nature to decide when labor commences.

Vaginal Exams

It impacts how labor progresses. There are other ways to determine how labor is progressing. Vaginal exams increase the risk of infection.

Enema

No medical indication that enemas are necessary.

Shaving

No medical indication that shaving is necessary.

Clothing Options

Be comfortable. Since oxytocin is a love hormone, consider a slinky gown. Hospital gowns do not provide the privacy needed. However, birth can be messy. It might be nice to be able to return the gown once labor is over.

Positions of Choice

Women need to feel uninhibited during labor. Positioning can facilitate the baby descending.

Questions Directed to the Birthing Companion

Mother can focus on what her body wants rather than considering what forms the care provider needs to complete.

Dim Lights

It helps the mother relax.

Music

It helps the mother relax by releasing endorphins.

Aromatherapy

It helps the mother relax by releasing endorphins.

Nurse Partial to Natural Birth

Will be more supportive of the birthing couple.

Water/Food

Women need food and water for their bodies to function appropriately during labor. The body is working; it needs to be hydrated and be given light snacking to maintain energy.

Privacy

Mandatory for labor to progress smoothly and gently.

Control and Respect

Discuss all interventions offered/suggested and consider all alternatives.

EFM (External Fetal Monitoring)

Studies indicate that continuous monitoring only increases the risk of cesarean.

Bath or Shower

Calming, relaxing, and minimizing discomfort.

Pain Relief Options

Research all the pros and cons of each option.

Episiotomy

Studies clearly state the ease of recovery from a tear versus a cut. Women who give birth in an upright position and breathe the baby down versus directed pushing that minimizes tearing risk.

Catching the Baby

Who would like to receive baby as they emerge? Birth companion? Mother?

Birthing of Baby

Allow the baby to emerge without assistance. The care provider who assists the baby to turn increases the risk of tearing the perineum.

Discovery of Baby's Sex

If unknown, who has the privilege of announcing?

Suctioning

Studies show that babies will cough and clear any phlegm on their own unless there are unusual circumstances.

Cord Clamping

Studies now show that allowing the blood from the placenta to flow to the baby will decrease the risk of anemia. The placenta is a temporary organ and belongs to the baby. The baby has two-thirds of the blood supply in their body, and the rest is in the placenta.

Vernix

A natural bacterial barrier for the baby; babies tend to breastfeed easier if the vernix is left alone.

Birth of Placenta

Many care providers like to inject synthetic oxytocin to speed up the birth of the placenta and control the bleeding. The injection interferes with the hormones the mother's body produces after birth that in turn promotes bonding between mother and baby.

Placenta: Kept or Discarded

There are many options for the placenta. It can be left attached to the baby until it releases on its own—usually, three to four days postnatally. The placenta is covered with rosemary to control the bacteria and odor. It is carried around in a cloth bag or basket. If cut immediately, it takes seven to ten days for the cord to heal. If it is left on, it releases in three to four days.

Some doulas process and encapsulate the placenta, which the mother ingests, assisting in recovery.

There are recipes so the mother can eat the placenta, assisting in recovery.

Some parents like to bury the placenta under a tree as a tribute to the child's birthing.

Quiet so parents can bond with the baby and the baby can imprint on parents.

Babies want to bond with their parents and gently become aware of their surroundings outside the womb. The womb was quiet, warm, wet, dim, and tasted of the mother's diet. They would like a similar experience outside the womb as they transition into our world.

Vitamin K jab

Babies are born with low levels of vitamin K and a risk of hemorrhage. There is vitamin K in breast milk, which comes in day two or three. The amount of vitamin K in the jab is the adult dosage thought to be dangerously high.

Weighing of the Baby

Let the dad carry the baby over to the scale to ensure the baby's gentle treatment.

Breastfeeding

Do you want to breastfeed? Please see the newborn care guide section that follows for more information on breastfeeding.

Vaccines BCG / Hepatitis B

Vaccines are very controversial, and I encourage all parents to read all there is out there on the pros and cons and make an informed choice.

Moving to the Postnatal Ward

Request the use of the gurney to move to the postnatal ward. This way, the mother can hold the baby while lying down. Otherwise, they put the baby in a plastic cart and wheel them alongside. Babies do not need to go into the nursery for observation. Keep your baby with you. If the baby is with you, there is no way your baby can go home with the wrong parent.

Rooming-in

Your baby needs your comforting smell and touch to bond with you and your partner. Holding your baby stabilizes their heartbeat, breathing, and body temperature. Plus it stimulates the production of breast milk.

Family Bed

Having your older child in a trundle bed with you and your partner will help the bonding process of the family dynamics.

Postnatal Ward Routine Options

A postnatal ward is a busy place. Have someone visit you to check on your bleeding, check on the baby, take your food order, bring the food three times, take the food away three times, clean the room, take your vitals, and take the baby's vitals. It's a seemingly endless stream of "care." Consider asking the staff to limit their interruptions and not check on you during the 9:00 p.m. to 6:00 a.m. shift. Consider going home.

Cesarean Birth Options

General or spinal anesthesia.
Music.
Request no idle chatter.
Request positive intention behind the care provider's touch.
Immediate skin-to-skin contact with baby.
Delayed cord clamping.

The dad takes the baby out due to the cold room—can meet the mother in the recovery room.

NICU. The dad goes with the baby. Ask for LC for breast pump every three hours.

Allow the baby to crawl out of the womb on its own.

Well, honestly? Consider a home birth with a midwife if possible. As a doula, I quit attending hospital births, as everything their protocols required interfered with the labor progressing. Women birthed so much easier and gentler at home. There were no birthing centers in Singapore, so home birth or hospital were the only options.

IS IT TIME?

If you do choose a hospital birth, you have options. You can opt to go early in labor to make the hospital room your own, or you can go as late as possible so you can labor more comfortably at home. Not all women experience the same, and these are all normal occurrences.

There is no way I can tell you when you should go to the hospital. It will be up to you to decide. The longer you stay at home, the fewer interventions you will experience in the hospital. If you plan on medicalized pain relief options, you might want to go sooner.

Hopefully, you have discussed if you prefer to go early or late in labor. If you have chosen early, consider waiting until labor is well established. The surges should last at least sixty seconds long and be somewhere between three to five minutes apart consistently for an hour. Now that being your marker does not automatically mean you have chosen the perfect time.

If you have decided to wait until later in labor, consider waiting until the natural expulsive reflex kicks in. Most women bear down for over an hour—but not all do. The challenge with waiting this long is that it might be difficult for the mother to walk to the car, as the surges are very powerful.

SIGNS AND SYMPTOMS OF LABOR

The Braxton-Hicks contractions will become more frequent as you get closer to going into labor. Some women never feel them. This is the body's way of getting the uterus ready for labor. You don't even have to go to the gym. The body does the workout for you!

There is an increase in vaginal discharge to facilitate the easier descent of the baby.

A backache is the body's way of communicating with the mother to try a new position to labor in. Recruiting the birthing companion to massage is a good way to alleviate the discomfort.

Birth show. Some bleeding might occur.

Inward focus. Women tend to shut out all distractions. They look like they are daydreaming.

Movement. Women tend to rotate their hips and/or squat. This is intuitive and should be encouraged or validated.

Noise. Some women make moaning or growling noises. It's intuitive and should be encouraged or validated.

Loss of confidence. This is a hormonal change, and the mother should be supported compassionately.

Nausea. Consider peppermint essential oils to minimize discomfort.

Water releases usually occur at 7 to 8 cm.

Transitioning between feeling hot and cold.

Pressure to bear down as the baby descends into the birth path.

The labor surges become quite regular for some and start somewhere between three to twenty minutes apart and last thirty to forty-five seconds. This is early labor.

They progress to two to ten minutes apart and last sixty to eighty seconds. Labor is well established.

Usually, the surges progress to two to five minutes apart and last ninety seconds. This is definitely your time to go to the hospital unless you plan for a home birth.

Then as you breathe your baby down, two to five minutes apart—or no time between—and sixty to ninety seconds long.

As a doula, I depended on the two to five minutes apart until a mother blew away my paradigm and experienced surges never closer than ten minutes apart and never lasted longer than sixty seconds as she breathed her baby down and out. These are all averages, and no one should expect their labor to be exactly like this. You might not experience all the norms, only some of them, and the timings for you might be unique.

Do keep in mind that you never know exactly what will happen, and prepare yourself to ask the questions necessary to ensure you understand all your options to make an informed choice.

QUESTIONS ABOUT INTERVENTIONS

Have the birthing companion ask the following questions, as the mother will be focusing on her baby and body.

Benefits: What are the benefits of the interventions you are offering?

Risks: What are the risks of the interventions you are offering?

Alternatives: What alternatives are there?

Intuition: Use your intuition to decide which is your best option.

Nothing: What happens if we do nothing?

Time: How much time do we have to make a decision?

Asking all these allows you to make an informed decision.

The birthing companions always want to know what they can do to help. Trust me, the role is essential! The mother's role—labor and birth. The birth companion (BC) does everything else. Please note that this is for healthy women with healthy babies, and you want a birth that maternity care providers do not chronologically manage. Do not interpret this as medical advice. Below is all you need to know to support a woman through labor.

SIGNS OF LABOR COMMENCING

Increase in Warm-up Surges

The body knows that the uterine muscle needs to be strong for labor. Without any effort from the mother, the warm-up surges prepare the uterine muscle. Isn't the female body amazing? The abdomen simply tightens with no regular pattern or timing.

Baby's Head Engages

Somewhere between thirty-two to thirty-seven weeks, the baby moves down into the pelvic inlet. Prior to the baby's head engaging, there is no room for the mother to eat and breathe comfortably. As the baby's head engages, the baby will now be sitting further down on the bladder, increasing the need to urinate.

Uterine Seal Releases

The uterine seal might release two weeks before the birthing day. It's a thick discharge and might be greenish, tinged with pink. It might come out in little bits or a larger clump. It might not come out at all, disengaging only as the baby descends.

Surges become Rhythmic

There might be many days of the surges or tightening before birthing, but they come in a very regular pattern. As labor progresses, they last longer and longer and get closer and closer together.

Birth Show

There might be some bleeding as the cervix softens and opens. It might be as heavy as a period flow.

Water Releases

Unlike how movies dramatize birth, this usually occurs between 7 and 10 cm during advanced labor—only 5 percent release before labor. As long as the waters are clear and not tinged green, it should be okay to wait for labor to start.

MOTHER'S ROLE DURING LABOR

Labor.
Birth.
Follow her body's lead.
The birth companion caters to her every need.

HORMONES OF LABOR

Relaxin. This hormone allows the mother's body to help the baby easily move down the birth passage.

Loosens ligaments and joints.

Softens bones and cartilage.

Smooths the wall of the vagina to allow the baby to pass through the pelvis.

Weakens the amniotic sac.

Oxytocin. This is a love hormone, the same hormone your body creates when making love. Oxytocin increases with the following:

Love

Privacy

Warmth

Feeling safe

Loss of inhibition

Endorphins. The feel-good hormone that eases the discomfort of labor. The following increases the production of endorphins:

Hypnosis

Laughter

Breath work

Massage

Aroma

Music

Color

Chocolate

Movement

Natural Expulsive Reflex

The mother's body will push the baby out with an overwhelming urge to bear down. Women in a coma give birth, so consider allowing the mother to direct the pushing effort. Breathing the baby down reduces the risk of tearing and birthing in an upright position versus lying down.

She might feel shaky, nauseated, the transition between hot and cold, become inwardly focused, and lose confidence.

Peppermint essential oil helps with nausea.

Massage helps with shakiness as well as calming breathing techniques.

Support the temperature transitions with warm blankets or cold washcloths as needed.

Do not interrupt the inward focus.

Allow the mother to pay attention to her innate knowledge.

Encourage the mother with positive affirmations.

BIRTH THE BABY WANTS

Mother-directed pushing: The mother's body instinctively knows how to ease the baby out. The force-directed pushing increases the risk of tearing and bleeding heavily post-birth. It is also a gentler descent for the baby.

Emerging without interference: Babies instinctively know how to turn as they move through the pelvic inlet and outlet. Outside interference increases the risk of tearing the perineum.

Warmth: It is quite wet and warm in the womb; they want to emerge into a warm environment. It facilitates the baby to regulate their body temperature.

Dim lights: it is quite dim in the womb, and it eases their transition into our world.

Soft sounds: the womb sounds are muted, so soothing, quiet sounds outside ease the baby's transition into their new surroundings.

Pleasant aroma: The womb provides a soft scent of the mother's diet and amniotic fluid. Harsh chemical smells in a hospital are challenging for a new baby.

Skin-to-skin contact: This is a wake-up call to the baby's brain. This tactile stimulus helps form connections to the forebrain. It also stabilizes the baby's heartbeat, temperature, and breathing.

Delayed cord clamping: Studies are now showing that the blood in the placenta belongs to the baby. Only two-thirds of the baby's blood supply is in their body at birth; the other one-third of the baby's blood transfers within approximately ten minutes following birth.

Leave the vernix alone. The vernix is a natural bacteria barrier. Do not wipe the baby dry. It also facilitates the baby finding the breast via the breast crawl. Placing the baby on the mother's abdomen, the baby will crawl within one hour and self-attach to the breast. This process is also a wake-up call to the baby's brain, creating connections between the fore- and hindbrain. Consider bringing your soft towels and blankets to the hospital rather than using their white, rough, and bleached terry towels.

Don't let the baby out of your sight. There is no need for a healthy baby to go to the nursery for observation. Keep your baby with you to bond, facilitate milk production, and help the baby's immune system; and no one can send your baby home with the incorrect parents.

Hold your baby. Babies do not want to be with anyone but their parents. We are the only species that tries to separate babies from their mothers. Babies belong with their mothers.

Talk to your baby. Your baby has been listening to you since twenty-four weeks inside the womb; they want to hear you and see you, putting a face to your voice. They can focus on your face if they are within six to twelve inches away.

BIRTH COMPANION'S ROLE

Keeper of the birth plan: keep the progression to the plan unless changes are needed.

Interface with midwife or other maternity care staff: helps the mother to be inwardly focused and follow her body's lead.

Hypnosis prompts: Helps the mother remain calm and relaxed. Bonus! It helps produce endorphins, the feel-good hormone.

Massage: releases endorphins, relaxes the mother, and provides relief from any discomfort.

Aromatherapy: releases endorphins and provides relief as labor progresses. Seek the advice of an aromatherapist on which aromatic oils to use for each progression of labor.

Wearing chosen birth and relaxation color: anchors the mother into her relaxation.

Ensure mother has the privacy she needs: allows her to follow her innate knowledge and produce oxytocin and eases and hastens the progression of labor.

Humor: releases endorphins.

Assistance with breath work: releases endorphins and eases and hastens the progression of labor.

In charge of the music: releases endorphins and follows the mother's moods.

Ensure mother is hydrated and well-fed: allows the muscles to function properly, as dehydration is avoided, and provides energy as required.

Assist in laboring positions: see the different positions used during labor and why you would want to use them earlier in the book.

Encourage the mother to breathe the baby down rather than force pushing: eases the baby's progression through the birth passage and minimizes the risk of tearing and heavy bleeding following the birth.

Provide a warm blanket or cold washcloths.

Peppermint essential oil for nausea.

Ensure her ability to remain inwardly focused without interference.

Provide reassurance.

Ensure immediate skin-to-skin contact.

Bring along a baby towel to use rather than the rough, overbleached terry towels used in hospitals.

Birth is a once-in-a-lifetime opportunity. I hope you take the time to research, envision, and create a beautiful birth experience for you and your baby.

BIRTH VIDEO LINKS

Find the ones that make you feel comfortable and empowered. Find the ones that you like. Watch them repeatedly to ingrain it in your head so that when your labor starts, your body follows your vision. I apologize for almost all these being water births. I could not find any land births that were this lovely.

https://vimeo.com/44227035?fbclid=IwAR3gpZXIgaJ91vlb-dydca4Ij-WDR1a_H2gdTjlEekZp6Ao1V45lD-hybV8U

HypnoBirthing Home Water Birth

I love how this video shows how the dad "labors" as much as the mom does. It's incredible how this baby swims out! No pushing whatsoever to aid this baby emerging.

https://vimeo.com/266582511?ref=fb-share&sfns=mo&fb-clid=IwAR1QUC2OWNxfA6jq1UELMLqU1IsD6UsHYCUv5cT-pwUUORb71vRVDGeFYG8c

Home Birth: Second Baby Water Birth with Lots of Affirmations

This baby is also breathed gently into being. The water is also very clear, as relaxed and gentle births have minimal bleeding. I love how the sister is so calm and happy about the birth.

https://www.youtube.com/watch?v=zj_d7fSyV8k

Second Baby Water Birth in a Birthing center

This family's bonding is lovely to observe and, again, gently breathing the baby out, clear water, and the gorgeous first eye contact between mother and babe.

https://www.youtube.com/watch?v=a_hqvRrLQ8k

Hospital Water Birth: Their First Baby

It's lovely to see this first-time mother be so inwardly focused, following her body's lead to birth her baby. Even after the midwife places the baby on her chest, this mother is still "somewhere else." I love the dad's first eye-to-eye bonding with his new baby—a tribute to HypnoBirthing.

https://www.youtube.com/watch?v=nX84oztuato

Home Water Birth with Lots of Vocalizing

This second-time mother finds that vocalizing helps her remain inwardly focused and relaxed. Notice how gentle the midwives are with this gorgeous wee one.

https://www.youtube.com/watch?v=qlGnCsz-Q7M&list=PL23E46D072F3F94D1&index=18

Home Water Birth

This first-time mother is sensual in her movements as she labors and her positioning as she births this gorgeous, sweet baby.

http://www.rightthisminute.com/video/rtmtv-new-birthing-process-allows-newborn-babies-walk-world?=rtmsoc&fbclid=IwAR0DzOIoZ4Lir0dY5gdUXVNVSz8uE5l7i-jflR36WXpL4ZGGbUAJzmXsfSk

SECTION 8

Newborn Care and Breastfeeding

Providing baby skin-to-skin contact at birth aids in stabilizing their temperature, stabilizing their heartbeat and blood pressure, and having higher blood sugar levels. They are less likely to cry and to breastfeed longer. Babies are hardwired to latch on and latch on well within the first two hours following birth. If the baby is laid midline on the mother's chest, the baby will crawl and bob his/her head to self-attach on the breast. The mother's body is the perfect habitat for the newborn. If the baby is cold, the maternal temperature will rise to the appropriate level to keep the baby warm. If the mother is busy with birthing the placenta or if she did tear a bit and needs stitches, I encourage the birth companion to remove their shirt so the baby can have the skin-to-skin contact.

What do newborns need?

Mother's milk

Love

Warmth

Security

Babies are born with all five senses. They are aware of their birth experience. How you care for them right from the start will cause synapses to fire in the brain and affect how they will learn their entire lives.

Human babies are born somewhat prematurely as far as brain development goes compared to other mammals. If human babies had the same brain capacity at birth as a chimpanzee, women would be pregnant for two years and the head would be too large for us to birth them. Synapses are firing for the first two years of life and that period of time brings babies to that level.

If the baby is taken away from mother or maltreated, there are more hindbrain connections made—the old hindbrain—which is how they keep themselves safe and survive. Skin-to-skin contact with parents creates more forebrain connections. The baby feels safe and creative development occurs.

DUNSTAN BABY LANGUAGE

An Australian woman, Priscilla Dunstan, has a photographic memory for sound. When she was five years old, she could listen to Mozart once and play it note for note on her violin. As an adult, she performed in opera as a mezzo-soprano. When her son was born, she heard the patterns in his cries and was able to determine the meaning. Years of studies—including all nationalities and in several different countries, cultures, and languages—found that there are universally five distinct cries related to physical needs.

Hearing and understanding these cries aid parents in meeting their baby's needs quickly and satisfying them, keeping everyone happier. I encourage all parents to take a Dunstan Baby Language class and, at the very least, download the app.

Here are the five basic baby needs that provide security and comfort for your newborn: mother's milk, burping, clean diapers and comfortable temperature, assistance in eliminating lower wind, and sleep.

Babies do not know how to do these on their own. Their cries are their way of communicating with you in order to get their needs met. According to Dunstan Baby Language, by listening at the beginning of the communication—before the cry moves into a full-blown wail—their needs are met quickly, creating a much quieter environment and contentment for all.

You can change the baby's position to hear their cry more precisely if you cannot figure out which cry is occurring. If the baby is on your shoulder, try setting them in your lap or over your knees. If you still cannot figure out the cry, go through the checklist—nappy, burp, lower wind, and tiredness. The purpose of understanding the cries is for parents to respond quickly and appropriately to the baby's cries so there is less crying, more sleep, and everyone is happier.

The cries are in response to a physical need; it is the old hindbrain, creating a physical reaction to the needs, resulting in a verbal cue. When babies are hungry, the old hindbrain triggers the sucking reflex, and the tongue is at the top of the mouth. When they are tired, it is the yawn reflex. When they need to burp, the baby's chest tightens as they try to get the air to come up.

Your baby's personality is present right from the start, and it is recognizable from the activity in the womb. You might not get the character you have been dreaming of and will need to adjust accordingly. Be accepting of who your baby is.

MILK

For how long would you like to breastfeed? WHO recommends exclusive breastfeeding for the first six months, then introduce solids and continue to breastfeed for two years and beyond. Planning to breastfeed is more powerful and creates more effortless success rather than trying to breastfeed.

Benefits of Breastfeeding

The mother:

Prolactin for bonding, calming, mothering, and milk production.

Oxytocin for bonding and uterus surges, returning the uterus to its original size.

Bonding: Oxytocin is a love hormone and connects mother and baby. By burping, bathing, calming, walking, and nappy changing, the partners can relieve the mothers of the entire responsibility of baby care and provide her the rest time she needs. The baby needs to learn unconditional love without food involvement. Partners need to discover their way and have permission to interact with the baby in their style. Mothers should be careful not to direct how the partner picks up the baby or burps the baby. Let the partners do it their way. Studies show that the partners will spend more time with their babies if they can find their parenting style.

Mobility: no formula nor bottles to carry about. The breast is always there and ready.

Always the right temperature: no need to heat formula in bottles.

Lowers risk of certain cancers.

Returns body into shape quicker.

Period cycle delay, less fertile: does *not* eliminate fertility.

More sleep: as parents are not preparing formula.

Lower libido: I encourage couples to talk about this now. Partners will need to woo their wives like they did when first dating. Mothers expend more energy whilst breastfeeding than when the babe was in the womb. Since babies feed every two to three hours and might take up to an hour at each feeding, it leaves little time for the desire to be present.

Older babies can touch base; soothe them when distressed or when they have owies. Some mothers are comfortable being used as a pacifier. Other mothers are not. Some babies need more comfort sucking than others. All are simply variations of normal.

The partner:

More sleep: If the baby is sleeping near the mother, she will usually wake up just before the baby does. Babies will usually lick their lips, fist at their mouth, root for a breast, and then cry. The baby does not even need to cry if the mother picks the baby up and feeds immediately. The partner never needs to wake up. She will get more rest, as she never truly has to awaken completely if the baby is within reach.

Peace of mind: The partner knows what the baby is getting. I encourage parents to review the ingredients in formula.

Mobility: nothing to carry about with you.

Fewer doctor bills: baby will be healthier.

The baby:

Fewer allergies: helps build the baby's immunity to allergic reactions.

Immune system: There is communication between the composition of the mother's milk and the baby. Let's say your mother-in-law takes the baby out for a walk in the stroller. Someone says, "Oh, what a cute baby!" and then sneezes on your baby. The baby comes back to the mother and latches on, and the milk will adjust to fighting off that to which the baby was exposed. The mother does not even have to be exposed. Milk cures everything! Pink eye? A little breast milk in the affected eye.

Normal IQ: A study with preterm babies proved that those fed formula had lower IQ by five points. Breastfed babies have normal IQs, as formula is not the natural way of feeding babies.

Jaw development: The baby needs to suckle to get the milk to flow. It helps them develop their jaw muscles and form the palette.

Weight control as an adult: because there is so much sugar in formula, adults have a more challenging time maintaining their proper weight when formula-fed.

Happier: healthier and better gut development aids in happier babies.

More sleep: again, gut development helps them sleep better and experience less colic.

Healthier: perfect nutrition and immunity.

Gut development: easier to digest for a baby and helps the gut develop the proper bacteria.

Bonding: Oxytocin helps the baby to bond with mother. They love eye contact and interaction when breastfeeding.

Perfect nutrition: the communication between mother's milk and baby again. The milk changes as the baby's needs change (growth spurt, milk adapts; brain development, milk changes). Formula never changes. It is always the same.

Always the right temperature: babies can have their needs met quickly.

The environment:

Overall, less carbon footprint.

Less water.

Less manufacturing.

Less packaging.

Less transportation.

Less medical care.

However, it would negatively impact formula industry income. Many jobs would be lost if everyone breastfed. Many countries are now limiting hospitals from sending formula home. The formula industry is shifting to manufacturing a mother's formula. They are attempting to create a market for new mothers to a purchase their supplement. The promotion is their product will enhance her breast milk nutrition value. They are also starting to target older babies.

Here is a link to a great article about milk production and human consumption: http://www.mindbodygreen.com/0-10998/the-sour-facts-about-milk-what-every-parent-needs-to-know.html

In the second year of your baby's life (twelve to twenty-three months), 448 ml of breast milk provides the following:

29 percent energy requirements

43 percent protein

36 percent calcium

75 percent vitamin A

76 percent folate

94 percent vitamin B12

60 percent vitamin C

Composition of Breast Milk

Colostrum: This is the baby's first immunization and aids in moving meconium through, reducing the risk of high levels of jaundice. The more colostrum the baby has, those first few days will help the baby gain weight rather than lose weight the first week. It will also aid in the milk coming in quicker. Because the baby's stomach is so tiny, if you were to express the colostrum, you would only see tiny dots of it on the tip of your nipple.

Foremilk: thirst-quenching.

Hind milk: Calorie-rich milk comes at the end of the feed. This milk will satisfy the baby's hunger.

Once the milk comes in, many mothers feel a tingling in their breasts as it begins to flow. A milk ejection reflex will spray the milk across the room if the baby pulls away from the breast.

Always empty one side before offering the other so the baby can get the hindmilk, satisfying the baby's hunger. The baby will gain weight and be more content.

Baby should self-detach: Never detach the baby from the breast and offer the other breast only after the baby finishes the first breast. The next feed would start on the other breast. An excellent way to remember which breast to use is to have a bracelet (switching from wrist to wrist), a hair tie, or a ring.

Breast compression: Babies born after epidurals and cesareans or other drugs tend to be sleepy. There are ways to help the baby stay awake to ensure they get the nutrition they need. One is breast compression. Thumb and fingers on opposite sides of the areola, pressing toward the breastbone and then inward to cause milk to flow into the baby's mouth, waking them up. Another is to tickle the baby's hands and feet, stroke the baby's jawline, and remove their clothes so they are not so warm and toasty that they fall asleep.

There is no need to schedule times to feed. Some babies are efficient feeders done in ten minutes, while others take an hour. Some babies are cluster feeders. They feed every two hours for three feeds, then sleep for five hours, and then three feeds every two hours. Other babies are feeding exactly every 1.5 hours around the clock. All scenarios are typical.

More breastfeeding in the first few days means more milk later.

It takes thirty to forty days to establish a milk supply.

At one month, the mother will produce just about as much milk per day as the baby will need.

Some babies like to use the mom's breast as a pacifier. Breasts can be comfort as well as a food supply. Lactation consultants recommend avoiding pacifiers and other types of artificial nipples for at least the first three to four weeks. Most breastfed babies—if they get a pacifier at all—would be better off without a pacifier until the mom's milk supply is well established (six to eight weeks, usually) and the six-week growth spurt is over. That way, you've established an adequate milk supply and haven't lost any much-needed breast stimulation to a pacifier.

Breastfeeding reduces your fertility but does not eliminate it. Please discuss with your partner what your options are for contraception.

After birthing, you will have bleeding for three to six weeks. This blood loss is called lochia. It will be heavy in the first few days and perhaps even release a few blood clots. It diminishes to a normal period flow and then to a brownish discharge. After the lochia stops, parents can reinitiate their sex life. Both of you will be tired; however, remember that oxytocin builds bonding and relaxation. Have patience with each other.

Some mothers need a break now and again. Don't be surprised if, when the partner comes home from work one day, the mother hands over the baby, takes the keys, and drives off. She is usually back in one hour. She just needs to get away. With all the two-hour feeds, baths, attempting to rest and feed herself, and taking a shower now and again, mothers can be easily overwhelmed. If the mother feels like her crying infant is simply too much, put the baby down and walk away. Take some calming breaths, and call for help if needed.

Maintain your life's interests. Babies need well-rounded parents for them to grow up well-rounded. If the partner likes to golf every weekend pre-baby, that might be okay in one family to continue; but in another, the partner will be reducing that back to fewer outings. I encourage parents to discuss this before the birth to be better prepared and avoid miscommunications later.

There is no need to use sterilizing tablets or other products. The baby is already used to the bacteria in your household. Many people tend to overclean with Lysol. Our bodies need exposure to bacteria for our immune system to grow.

Breastfeeding tops provide easy access for breastfeeding, making life simpler. Consider organic cotton for not only the tops but also for the nursing pads. Reusable nursing pads are easier on the nipples, with not as much sticking as paper ones. In the beginning, when the milk flows, both breasts have a letdown, and pads are essential to avoid wet spots on your clothing. For some, after a while, the body adjusts and the milk flows only on one side. And by the way, leaking breasts add a whole new element to lovemaking. Nursing bras should have no underwires, as these can cause clogged milk ducts. Massaging the breasts can help reduce the risk of clogged milk ducts.

Using two fingers, press down at the noon position on the breast and massage in a circle. Then at one o'clock, then at two o'clock, all the way around twelve. Use flat fingers (the first two) and rub up and down next to the areola and then above and below the areola. The mother should do this several times a day.

Make sure you tell the doctor that you are breastfeeding when they are prescribing medication. Then go home and google it. Make sure you are comfortable with taking it and understand the effects on your baby.

Can women drink while breastfeeding? Usually, alcohol—one glass of wine—will be processed through our bodies in one hour. So you can feed the baby and then have a glass of wine. Only 2 percent of the alcohol in the mother's body reaches breast milk. If you are sober enough to drive, you should be able to breastfeed. Many professionals recommend that mothers stop drinking when they are breastfeeding. Newborn's livers are not yet functioning at 100 percent, so it will stress the baby to process the alcohol in the breast milk.

Ensure you use a deodorant that does not have aluminum or other toxic chemicals that might leak into the milk supply.

As long as you eat spicy foods throughout your pregnancy, they should be okay once the baby is born—the flavors of what you are eating pass through into the milk. Try to avoid foods that make you windy.

Around days three through five, when the milk comes in to replace the colostrum, there is a hormonal shift in the woman's body.

This hormonal shift might trigger what is known as baby blues. Mothers might cry for no apparent reason, be short-tempered, lose sleep even though tired, lose their appetite, and feel disconnected from their baby. This abnormality usually clears within twenty-four to seventy-two hours. If it continues, please seek professional help. Don't let the mother slide into a depression. Babies can also become depressed. Partners, be patient, be supportive. Make sure the mother is getting enough rest and eating well. Vitamin B is a mood stabilizer, and staying hydrated is critical to establishing and keeping the milk supply.

Mothers should call for breastfeeding support at the first sign of challenges.

These Are What Might Get in the Way of Successfully Breastfeeding

We don't see others breastfeeding, and we learn by observation. Women have special rooms next to the toilet; they have drapes to cover themselves, so there is no viewing. There is a subconscious association with breastfeeding being wrong as we need to "hide."

The nurses in the hospitals come in, shove the baby on the breast, check the latch, and then leave. The mother has learned nothing. She should tell the nurse to talk her through how to latch the baby. Otherwise, she goes home, and there is no one to put the baby on her breast.

Babies go through growth spurts. A feeding schedule has been established for a while, and the baby feeds every two hours. One morning, the baby is latching every thirty minutes. Pediatricians often advise mothers that they don't have enough milk and top it up with formula. The mother should consider simply staying in her jammies all day and feeding until her supply catches up. My suggestion is to always check with a lactation consultant.

Family members are not always supportive of breastfeeding. Perhaps let the family know in advance that you will be breastfeeding. This is your choice, and you request that they be supportive. Consider asking other family members to attend your classes on breastfeeding, so they learn the benefits of breast milk versus formula. Whoever is related to this family member is responsible for the communication of correcting the attitude. Otherwise, the spouse does not feel supported.

Don't light a candle at both ends. Mothers need to get plenty of rest for their bodies to produce milk. The calorie intake is increased to 2,500 calories a day for the body to produce milk. New parents should recognize that it is not the time for Facebook. When the baby rests, the mother rests.

Self-care. Do take time for yourself. Go for a facial, pedicure, massage, or tea with your lady friends.

More milk out means more milk made. The more you breastfeed, the more milk your body will create.

Newborn babies feed twelve to eighteen times a day—every 1.5 to 2 hours. Babies are born waterlogged, so they have a supply to keep themselves hydrated for the first few days.

Rooming-in can help establish successful breastfeeding. The baby has more access to the breast, the quicker the milk comes in.

Crying is a late sign of hunger. They have other cues indicating hunger—rooting, putting a hand to their mouth, and licking their lips.

According to a Japanese study, more feeds in the first twenty-four hours correlated to less weight loss, more stools, less jaundice, and more significant milk intake on days two, three, and five.

How Do You Know if the Baby Is Getting Enough Milk?

Where there is input, there is output.

One wet nappy, one poo first day.

Two wet, two poo day two.

Three wet, three poo day three.

On day six, six wets and three poos mean the baby is not dehydrated. The more the merrier! Parents might see twice the amount of nappies! (Yes, lots of nappies every day is a good sign of a healthy baby.)

Weight gain indicates they are getting enough milk.

Baby is content, and they rest better.

Please make sure they treat your baby gently and compassionately in the hospital and move slowly with the baby. Request they talk to your baby and use your baby's name, tell your baby what they are doing and why.

Points to Note

The baby should be tummy to mommy's tummy when breastfeeding. If the baby is lying face up, they would have to turn their head to the side. And no one drinks turning their head to the side.

The mother's nipple should be on the baby's soft palette. Try running your tongue back on the roof of your mouth until you reach the soft palette. The baby needs to get enough of the breast into the mouth, so the nipple is at the soft palette.

If the mother is experiencing pain, the latch is not correct. Break the latch with the little finger and try again.

Mom needs to be relaxed and well-rested for good milk production and feeds.

Common Breastfeeding Challenges

Mastitis is the inflammation of the breast. Symptoms include the following:

Lump in breast
Red patch
Hot and swollen
Pus, pain flaring
Flu-like symptoms
Fever

Thrush is a yeast infection.
Intense pain in the nipple or breast
White spots on the nipples and in the baby's mouth or tongue
Red shiny nipples
Vaginal thrush infection
Seek medical attention for both of the above.

To Avoid Mastitis and Thrush

Ensure there is a good latch, and feed the baby frequently. Ensure the mom is hydrated and massaging the breasts regularly throughout the day; a manual pump can be useful. Avoid yeast products and sugar, and take a probiotic or acidophilus.

Engorgement

Feed baby often.

Express some of the milk to gain relief and aid the baby's ability to latch.

Use a warm washcloth that would allow the milk to flow.

Use ice to reduce swelling.

Cold cabbage leaves in the bra help eliminate some of the excess milk. The mother must be careful to remove the cabbage after some relief or it will draw out all the milk and ensure that the cabbage does not touch the areola.

Breastfeeding Visualization Exercise

Provided below is an excellent breastfeeding visualization. Have someone read this slowly to you as you sit comfortably, arms and legs uncrossed, and gently close your eyes. Breathe in deeply and breathe out four or five times, then return to normal breathing.

Get in a comfortable position and close your eyes. Let them shut comfortably, relaxing all the little lines around the eyes; and let that relaxation flow down, down your face, jaw, neck, shoulders, arms, hands, and fingers. Let your breathing and abdomen be soft and relaxed. Feel that relaxation drift down through your back and your pelvis, softening out any tension and letting it become ultra relaxed. Feel the relaxation now drift through your thighs, knees, calves, ankles, feet, and toes. Let your body just be at peace, rest, deeply relaxed now.

Now take some large, slow, deep breaths—slow breathing, allowing yourself to drift deeper and deeper into that comfortable, familiar, relaxed state. Find the most comfortable area in your body now and focus on that area. Feel how relaxed and at peace that part of you is. You want the rest of you to be that comfortable and deeply relaxed. So now, gently, as you breathe, let that feeling of complete comfort and relaxation just drift and radiate—maybe warmth, light, perhaps tingling vibrations, possibly even numbness, radiating out in all directions. Slowly up, down, and out—radiating and drifting, soothing all the muscles, fibers, cells, and molecules of your body and mind and spirit.

In a moment, we are going to go down the stairs of complete relaxation into the center of yourself. Picture yourself at the top of the safe stairs. Imagine these stairs. The details flood your mind now as you get ready to move down them. There are ten steps, and I will count them as you move twice as deep into relaxation with each step you go down.

One, twice as deep as before now.

Two, moving deeper into that beautiful relaxation.

Three, deeply, deeply relaxed.

Four, twice as deep now, relaxing, releasing.

Five, deeply comfortable, deeply relaxed.

Six, moving twice as deep now.

Seven, deeper into that wonderful relaxation.

Eight, twice as relaxed, drifting twice as deep.

Nine, doubling relaxation with every step-down.

Ten, doubling relaxation again, being more comfortable than ever before.

Now at the bottom of the stairs of complete relaxation, you see a beautiful door ahead of you that you know leads to the center of yourself. Go ahead and open the door and enter the room. Let the room's details unfold—the color of the room, the walls, the floor, the decorations, lighting, windows, plants, furniture. Just let it be what you need it to be—this safe, comfortable room inside yourself.

Go ahead now and find a comfortable chair and sit down. Let yourself be as comfortable as you would ever like to be. As you sit in this chair, you know that you can now talk to your baby. Picture your baby—inside the tiny home that is providing everything and taking away all that is unnecessary. Picture your baby now in the optimal position for birthing—back on your left front side, chin tucked to his chest, hands and feet so perfect, just enjoying the time to be with you, no requirements made of him right now and being at the center of you too. He knows your voice, your movements, your thoughts even. He can feel your emotions and is bathed with loving hormones as you send these loving, wonderful thoughts to your baby. Take a few moments to share any positive thoughts you may be having right now for your baby—sending your baby a love note right now. (Give extra time here.)

Now talk to your baby about breastfeeding; tell your baby you are looking forward to nourishing him at your breast. You know your baby is so smart that he will know how to breastfeed, know how to open up wide and where and how to place the tongue, and it will be so comforting to both you and your baby. Tell your baby how you both will be in a wonderful state of bonding during breastfeeding, just like you are now in a wonderful state of bonding. You look forward to the moments when you can hold your baby close, caressing his tiny body and watching your sweet baby take nourishment from you. Want it to happen, expect it to happen, and watch it happen.

Imagine now that you have had your baby and you are preparing for the first time your baby will nuzzle and feed at your breast. Imagine his little mouth, turning and opening and licking in response to a brush to his mouth or cheek. You hold your baby with his little warm tummy next to yours as you lovingly, gently direct his head and mouth to your breast. Your baby may need direction from you to help him find the areola surrounding the nipple.

See now how he opens his mouth with tongue down—opening wide and then latching onto your whole areola and beginning to draw in that wonderful golden liquid that provides sweet, concentrated nourishment to his body and spirit. Let your baby feel how wonderful it is to be warmed skin-to-skin with you, hearing your heartbeat as before, hearing your voice, but now seeing your loving face and feeling you touch his skin as he drinks the warm fluid that provides super immunity and loving care.

You feel your baby drawing your nipple into his mouth, and it comforts you to feel that gentle tug as your baby gains all he needs from you. You provide all the things your baby needs—warmth, comfort, warm milk, soft breasts, and loving words and glances.

Want it to happen, expect it to happen, and watch it happen.

Your body makes the perfect food for the baby that you are growing. Your body knows the baby; you are growing and will make milk perfectly designed for your baby. You are confident in your ability to provide this perfect food for your sweet baby. No matter what breast shape you have, you and your baby find a way to make breastfeeding work for both of you. You make the perfect amount of milk for your baby. Acknowledge that you can patiently overcome any special circumstances that may arise in breastfeeding your baby. Any road bumps with breastfeeding will be minor and easily corrected. With patience and love, you adjust and fine-tune your breastfeeding skills. Each feeding, you learn more and become more confident.

Picture again your baby opening wide, tongue down, and drawing in as much of the areola as he can, so the nipple is toward the back of his mouth. Want it to happen, expect it to happen, and watch it happen. Know, understand, and believe that this wonderful, empowering adventure awaits you. Take a moment to thank your body for the beautiful work it is doing and how it will continue to nurture your baby.

Take a few more moments to share these thoughts and love with your baby. I will now count up from five to one, and as I do, you become more aware of your surroundings. (Count up from five, four, three, two, one.) And when you are ready, open your eyes and stretch.

TIRED

There are many ways to aid the baby into sleep if they indicate they are sleepy. Tired shows itself as yawning, rubbing their eyes, and having heavy eyelids.

Rocking.

Patting.

Singing.

Birth ball bouncing.

Shushing.

Swaddling.

Swaying.

A quiet room to reduce the stimulation.

Please note: you cannot spoil a newborn.

Newborns are not sophisticated enough to manipulate parents. Other family members might try to influence parents that they are spoiling the baby.

Studies done in the 1970s found that if you pick a baby up within the first ninety seconds of crying, it will stop crying immediately. Sleep patterns do not occur until the baby is five to six months old; they will then sleep through the night for around five hours. Then the child will start teething and wake up throughout the night again. Or they might go through a growth spurt either physically or emotionally and need comforting—waking again. Babies do not consistently sleep through the night until they are two years old.

Each child is an individual, so don't try to compare your child to another. Babies know that mother means survival and will sleep longer when near or in their mother's arms. They will start to wake to see if their mother is near. If she is not, they will wake up thoroughly to ensure their survival. If the mother is near, they usually fall back asleep.

WIND IN THE TUMMY

Babies need to be burped throughout the day, not just after a feed. The birth ball is good for bouncing to aid the burp to come up.

Babies like the left shoulder due to the heartbeat on this side. It is a comforting reminder of when they were in the womb.

If you feed a baby and there is an air bubble in their tummy, that air bubble will come up (with the feed as spit up) or pushed down into the intestine as lower wind, which is commonly thought to be colic.

Newborns might take up to twenty minutes to burp until they get the hang of it and become quite efficient. Babies get the hang of it after a while, but the burp needs to be encouraged to come out initially.

Another sign of a baby needing to burp during a feed is that the baby will pull away from the breast, wiggle their little body, say, "Eh," and then try to latch back on, only to pull away again.

LOWER WIND

Lower wind can occur due to not burping your baby enough. Babies need to be burped often and have less lower wind so parents and babies can rest more easily.

There are many ways to help alleviate your baby's discomfort.

Place the baby with pressure on the tummy with your knee and rotate it around to help the wind out.

Gently press the baby's knees repeatedly to the chest until the wind comes out.

Place the baby draped over your forearm—supporting the head with your hand around the chin, tummy down—and massage the baby's back gently and firmly.

Gently massage the baby's tummy, starting with two fingers on the baby's right lower abdomen. Rub upward, then across to the other side, and then down, aiding the wind to come out.

When swaddling your baby, if they are windy, leave the feet free as windy babies like to kick.

The definition of colic is a baby who cries for three hours a day, three times a week over a three-week period. Consider medical advice if the baby does not respond to your ministrations listed above.

COMFORT

Babies might cry if they are either too hot or too cold. The perfect temperature is 24–25 degrees Celsius or 75–77 degrees Fahrenheit. If your environment is warmer, take clothes off; if cooler, put more clothes on.

Sometimes your baby just needs to change positions, and they need your help.

Your baby will need many nappy changes. Some babies do not like having a dirty nappy; others do not mind so much. When changing nappies, try not to lift the baby's bottom by lifting the feet. Turn the baby to the side slightly rather than lift the feet, as this stretches the back awkwardly and might cause muscle strain.

There are many nappy options. All have pros and cons, from branded disposables to organic disposables to cloth nappies. Do your homework and consider not only the convenience but also the costs involved and the impact on the environment.

The first poo your baby will pass is meconium, a dark tar-like substance that might be difficult to remove from their bum. Around days three through five, you will see a change to a greenish poo that transitions into yellow seedy breast milk poo.

Baby girls should be wiped front to back. Boys wipe all around the scrotum but do not retract the foreskin.

There is no need for creams or powders unless there is a rash.

Do watch this lovely video on bathing babies: http://www.youtube.com/watch?v=OPSAgs-exfQ.

When bathing your baby, have everything ready and set out so the baby is never left unattended.

Ensure the bathing environment is free from draft, is warm enough, and that the tub is the same level as your waist so you are not bending over the tub and straining the back.

Keep bathing your baby safe.

The water level can be as deep or as shallow as you like.

Temperature: insert the elbow into the water to determine that the temperature is the same as your elbow.

Put a towel in the bottom of the tub to create a nonslip surface.

Never leave a baby unattended: turn off the phone, and don't answer the door.

You might opt not to have a baby bathtub, as they outgrow them quickly. You can climb into the tub with your baby, take the baby in the shower, or use the kitchen sink.

Because wet babies are slippery, grasp the baby by the shoulder so that your forearm supports the baby's neck and head.

Start washing your baby at the head, body, legs, and feet. Genitals are washed last. I don't suggest using soaps, as babies are not truly dirty. Consider organic soaps and shampoos.

Use wet facial pads (two—one for each eye) to wipe the baby's eyes from the inside to the outside corner to avoid pushing any infection or foreign object into the tear duct. Use one for each eye to prevent transferring anything from one eye to the other.

Using a wet washcloth, wash the face. Start with the forehead, bridge of the nose, cheeks, around the mouth, and under the chin.

Then around the ear, behind the ear, neck, arms, hands, and fingers.

Now the body. The umbilical cord can get wet, so pat it dry gently. When dressing, make sure that the baby doesn't have material or nappy rubbing against the umbilical cord.

Follow with the legs, feet, and toes.

Change the grasp on the baby to the other hand, and tilt the baby to wash the backside.

And finally, the genitals. Little girls wipe front to back; little boys wipe all around the scrotum and do not retract the foreskin.

Try top and tail as another bathing option. Only wash face and genitals rather than the full bath.

Nappy free time. Most babies love being naked, and since they are now naked from the bath, you can consider some free time.

STATES OF NEWBORN AWARENESS

According to *The Amazing Talents of the Newborn* by Marshall Klaus, MD, and Phyllis Klaus, MFT, LMSW, there are six states of awareness in your newborn.

There Are Two Sleep States

Active sleep is also known as REM sleep. Babies enter sleep in the REM state, which is the opposite of adults.

Quiet sleep: Babies transition into this sleep from the REM sleep, and you will only see an occasional startle. They stay in this phase for approximately fifteen to twenty minutes before returning to active sleep.

There Are Three Active States

Active alert: babies in this phase are moving their arms and legs, gaining attention from their parents.

Quiet alert: Babies have little body movement in this phase, but this is an excellent time to interact with your baby. Newborns in this quiet alert state have the ability to mimic their parents' facial expressions. Get approximately six to twelve inches from the baby, open your mouth, and stick out your tongue every six seconds or so. Watch as your baby responds by mimicking your open mouth and tongue extension. There will be times when the baby is not interested in doing so. If your baby looks away, they indicate that they are being overwhelmed, in which case, you should discontinue the interaction. Wait for your baby to reinitiate the engagement.

Crying: pay attention to the cries as instructed in Dunstan Baby Language.

And then Drowsiness

This is shifting into the sleep state.

https://www.youtube.com/watch?v=fQmVKYp-hO0

I encourage you to enjoy your baby. Yes, you will be exhausted in the first few weeks following the birth of your baby. Take the time to follow your baby's cues and care for yourself. I have found the best advice for a new mother:

1. Feed and care for your baby.
2. Take care of yourself.

Have either your partner or a friend or a helper do everything else.

EPILOGUE

My wish is that you create empowering birth experiences for you and your baby(ies). The beginnings of life matter in how we live our lives, interacting with each other with love or fear.

I've spent decades clearing the early emotions that have created physical and emotional challenges in my life. I am blessed now to live in a beautiful home situated in stunning landscapes. I'm able to travel the world, experiencing and embracing different cultures and environments.

I am still challenged and continue to educate myself by seeking support in overcoming the effects of sexual abuse. I am confident I can obtain my goals of healthy habits and healing my body and mind.

I spend much of my time continuing to learn about fertility, pregnancy, labor, birth, and newborns. I share my knowledge freely. I encourage you to find your inspiration in life, living contentedly.

SOURCES OF INFORMATION

American Academy of Paediatrics, Policy Statement. *Breastfeeding and the Use of Human Milk*. Section on Breastfeeding. Published online February 27, 2012, Pediatrics, Vol. 129, No. 3. March 1, 2012, pp. e827–e841 (doi: 10.1542/peds.2011-3552).

APPPAH. https://birthpsychology.comCassidy, Tina. *The Amazing History of How We Are Born: Birth.*

Dewey, Kathryn G., PhD. *Nutrition, Growth, and Complementary Feeding of the Breastfed Infant.* 2001.

Grummer-Strawn, Laurence M., PhD; and Mei, Zuguo, MD, Pediatrics. *Does Breastfeeding Protect Against Paediatric Overweight? Analysis of Longitudinal Data from the Centres for Disease Control and Prevention Paediatric Nutrition Surveillance System.* Vol. 113, No. 2. February 1, 2004 pp. e81–e86 (doi: 10.1542/peds.113.2.e81).

Heinig, M. Jane, PhD, IBCLC. *Part 1: The Evidence for Breastfeeding.* Volume 48, Issue 1, 1 February 2001, Pages 105–123, Breastfeeding 2001.

How to Sterilize Baby Bottles and Nipples. http://babyparenting.about.com/od/nutritionandfeeding/f/sterilizebottle.htm.

Breastfeeding and Alcohol. http://kellymom.com/bf/can-i-breastfeed/lifestyle/alcohol.

Breastmilk Storage and Handling. http://kellymom.com/bf/pumpingmoms/milkstorage/milkstorage/.

Jacobson, Sandra W., PhD; Chiodo, Lisa M., MA; and Jacobson, Joseph L., PhD, Pediatrics. *Breastfeeding Effects on Intelligence Quotient in 4- and 11-Year-Old Children.* Vol. 103, No. 5. May 1, 1999, pp. e71.

Labbok, Miriam H., MD, MPH, IBCLC. *Effects of Breastfeeding on the Mother.*

Learning About Breastfeeding and Skin-to-Skin Contact. http://www.unicef.org.uk/BabyFriendly/Resources/Guidance-for-Health-Professionals/Learning-about-breastfeeding/Skin-to-skin-contact/Lewis, Thomas, MD; Armini, Fari, MD; and Lannon, Richard, MD. *A General Theory of Love.*

Mandel, D; Lubetzky, R; Dollberg, S; Barak, S; and Mimouni, FB. *Fat and Energy Contents of Expressed Human Breast Milk in Prolonged Lactation.* Pediatrics. 2005 Sept; 116(3):e432-e435.

Mongan, Marie. *HypnoBirthing.*

Moore, ER; Anderson, GC; and Bergman, N. *Early Skin-to-Skin Contact for Mothers and Their Healthy Newborn Infants* (Review). The Cochrane Library 2009, Issue 1.

Poslaneic, Tasha. *Providing Care for Survivors of Sexual Abuse during Childbirth.* AWHONN 2017.

Roberts, Holly. *Your Vegetarian Pregnancy: A Month by Month Guide to Health and Nutrition.* Available at www.half.com, $5.99 + shipping. Somer, Elizabeth. *Nutrition for a Healthy Pregnancy.*

Sunderland, Margot. *The Science of Parenting.* DK Publishing 2006. https://www.who.int/health-topics/breastfeeding#tab=tab_1Tamaro, Janet. *Breastfeeding Basics: So That's What They're For!*

Ward, Elizabeth. *Pregnancy Nutrition, Good Health for You and Your Baby.* Available at www.half.com. *What Should I Know About Giving My Breastfed Baby a Pacifier?* http://kellymom.com/ages/newborn/newborn-concerns/pacifier/.

ABOUT THE AUTHOR

Di Bustamante, certified by Childbirth International (CBI), has taught childbirth and newborn care classes for twenty years. She is also a certified hypnotherapist specializing in fertility and childbirth. Di holds a pre- and perinatal psychology educator certificate from the Association for Prenatal and Perinatal Psychology and Health (APPPAH). As a doula, she has attended over one hundred births. Di was also faculty at the HypnoBirthing Institute and is a Dunstan Baby Language faculty member. She has trained medical professionals on safely attending water births and assisted ob-gyns to lower their cesarean rates.

Printed in the USA
CPSIA information can be obtained
at www.ICGtesting.com
CBHW031927090824
12961CB00009B/286

9 781637 843406